Unseen Hands
THAT LEAD THE WAY

PEARLY STANLEY

PAGE PUBLISHING, INC.
Conneaut Lake, PA

First originally published by Page Publishing 2021

ISBN 978-1-6624-4445-6 (pbk)
ISBN 978-1-6624-4447-0 (hc)
ISBN 978-1-6624-4446-3 (digital)

Printed in the United States of America

This book is dedicated to my precious Lord Jesus.
Every word and every thought are inspired by him. He
was leading and guiding each step of the way.

CHAPTER 1

(Jesus, friend of sinners) I am so glad that Jesus is my best and forever friend and that he is a friend to the sinners because I am a great sinner in need of a loving Savior. And for him, to love me is more than I can understand. But I am forever grateful of his eternal love. Jesus, you are the highest of the highest, and we are the lowest of the lowest, yet you have such love for us. You know us from the inside out, yet you call us the apple of your eye. You became sin for us that we could be sin-free. You bore the shame and guilt of the human race so that one day, by your grace, we can be partakers of your most holy place. Everything that you went through to save me, my Lord, was what I deserved. I am so sorry for the agonizing pain, shame, and blame that you went through for me, but I am forever grateful that you did not quit until my sin was paid in full.

Why do you love me so? I will never know. Thank you is the best that I can do. But it comes deep from the heart. You could have well said that you will give me what I fully deserve, and that is the death that you took for me.

> For the wages of sin is death; but the gift of God
> is eternal life through Jesus Christ our Lord.
> (Romans 6:23 KJV)

Instead, you freely give me what I don't deserve. That is grace unlimited and eternal life. My precious Lord Jesus, thank you so much for such love. How costly my sin was for you, my kind King. Thank you for everything. I will be forever and eternally grateful for your great sacrifice. My holy Father, thank you so very much for loving us so much that you gave your only begotten Son to be the Savior of the world.

All that I am and all that I will ever be, I owe it all to you. Please use me in whatever way you know best. And please don't allow me to refuse to serve you in any way. Surely, there is a work that I can do to hasten your soon return to let others know that you are the friend of sinners. You love us all so much, but you will not leave us the way you found us. Your love draws us to you, and your grace cleans us up. When we are not walking in the ways of God, then we will fall prey to the traps of the evil ones. No matter what pit life has thrown us into, Jesus, friend of sinners, will be there to pull us out.

When upon him we call, there is no way you can go that God is not already there waiting to help and rescue you. He is a very present help in trouble (Psalm 46:1 KJV). Sin will take you where you let it take you and keep you longer than you want to stay. You cannot break the chain of sin that binds you on your own. Only the precious blood of Jesus can wash away all your sin. Accept him today, and know that he is not only your Savior, but he is also your forever friend. No matter what you have done or where you have been, Jesus loves you so very much. Your lifestyle is not a surprise to him. He is the only one that knows everything about us and still loves us unconditionally. Oh, what a Savior he is. Jesus is waiting on us to surrender our all to him. He can do anything, but he will not do it without our permission.

He will not overrule your choice of free will. He loves you too much to do that. When you make the choice to call on him, he can and will dispatch all of heaven to your rescue. Jesus never promises a life without sorrows, grief, or pain. But he did promise that his grace can and will see us through it all.

> And he said unto me, My grace is sufficient for thee: for my strength is made perfect in weakness. Most gladly therefore will I rather glory in my infirmities, that the power of Christ may rest upon me (2 Corinthians 12:9 KJV)

Jesus is not a tyrant waiting for his children to slip and fall so that he could zap us out of existence. That, my friend, is a lie from the enemy himself. Please know that God is for us and not against us. He is loving, kind, and caring for all his creatures, but especially for you and for me. He bought us with a high price, not silver or gold for you see, that would not do. He spilled his precious blood upon a wooden tree to set the human race free.

There is nothing, absolutely nothing, else that he can do for you or for me. He went beyond the extra mile. He did what no one else can do. That makes him our creator, redeemer, sustainer, and forever friend. He is so worthy to be praised. Life as we know it is fast coming to an end. And we must make a decision on whose side we want to be on. Choose this day whom you will serve. I have made up my mind that I am on the Lord's side. I hope that you will do the same. The world can offer fortune, glamour, and fame. But only Jesus can give peace, joy, love, and eternal life. Sometimes, because of what sin has done to us, we feel inadequate to come to our precious Jesus for cleansing. But he is the only one that can remove the stain of sin. Nothing else will do. He looks upon this fallen human race with deep pity and longs to see his creatures in a land where sin can never touch them again. His heart breaks for those he loves so much.

Christ is indeed the greatest treasure that earth has received. He is not an entity that is disconnected from his fallen race. He cares about every little detail of our life. And he wants to dry every tear that falls from our eyes. He stands waiting at the door of our hearts for us to open the door and welcome him in. He wants to eat with us and talk with us. He wants to be our forever friend. Today, if you will open the door to him, he will gladly come in. And your life will never be the same again. But if he doesn't feel welcome, he will not stay.

Jesus wants to feel welcome in every room of our hearts, not just the ones that we want him to have. He must be the Lord of all or not the Lord at all. When we let him have his way in our heart, then he can and will make us like him. Again, that must be a free choice that one makes. To have Jesus as our best friend, we need no other. The time is fast approaching when all those that we love and thought that we could count on will forsake us, but not Jesus. He is our forever best friend. You could surely count on him. He is trustworthy. Please make him your friend today. Don't delay. Send him a friend invite. He will gladly accept.

Shining Bright No Matter What

It is so easy to praise God when all is going well. It is so easy to sing songs when the sun is shining bright and we are on the mountaintop. But oh, it is deep down in the valley below where my soul must draw near to the one who can comfort and cheer. With his loving arms around me, there is no need to fear. That valley of despair has now become a mountain of praise.

CHAPTER 2

<><><><><><><><><><><><><><><><><><><><><><><><><><><><><><><><><>

In His Presence

There is nothing like being in the presence of God. You have an awesome sense of peace, joy, and delight that you cannot get anywhere else.

> My presence will go with you, and I will give you
> rest. (Exodus 33:14 NKJV)

We cannot go through life without experiencing the presence of God, some time or another. To do so, you will have to have a heart of stone. But if you are willing, God said, that he can melt your heart of stone and give you a heart of flesh (Ezekiel 36:26 NIV). To be in his presence, the cares of life must be put aside for a while. And nothing else should matter while we are in his presence.

> Be still, and know that I am God: I will be exalted
> among the heathen, I will be exalted in the earth.
> (Psalm 46:10 KJV)

We must come aside and spend quality and quiet time with him. Then and only then, you will experience his holy presence like you never have before. You will be captivated by the joy of being in his holy presence. When you feel the cares of this world overpowering you, and it seems like joy, and life is just being drain out of you, please run back into his presence. He is waiting for you with open arms. This world is filled with much darkness and despair. Jesus wants us to come apart in quiet time with him before we fall apart from the cares of life. When you take time to seek God and to enjoy being in his presence, it makes us a much better person. We are more able to cope with all that is going on around us. Life situations may not change, but God will give us the peace and strength that we need to face all that comes our way.

We must make Jesus our number one priority always. Everything else is to be secondary. Spending time with Jesus is always time well spent. The weight of this world can and will bring you crashing down. Jesus, when he was on earth, always took time to be with his Father. He always had his quiet time of communion with the Father. If Jesus saw the importance of it in his day, how much more for us to today? If there is ever a time that we needed to be in God's holy presence, it is now. We will not regret one moment spent in his presence.

> Thou wilt shew me the path of life: in thy presence is fulness of joy; at thy right hand there are pleasures for evermore. (Psalm 16:11 KJV)

Once you have tasted being in his presence, you will never be the same again. You just have to keep going back for more and more. Being in God's holy presence can change the way you think, the way that you interact with others, and the way you live. There is no greater joy than to know that the great God of the universe wants to spend time with his created creatures. He knows that we are carrying burdens that only he can lighten. He welcomes us with open arms and bids us to sit at his feet as he lifts our burdens and give us his peace. Jesus said,

> At that time Jesus answered and said, I thank thee, O Father, Lord of heaven and earth, because thou hast hid these things from the wise and prudent, and hast revealed them unto babes. Even so, Father: for so it seemed good in thy sight. All things are delivered unto me of my Father:

and no man knoweth the Son, but the Father;
neither knoweth any man the Father, save the
Son, and he to whomsoever the Son will reveal
him. Come unto me, all ye that labour and are
heavy laden, and I will give you rest. Take my
yoke upon you, and learn of me; for I am meek
and lowly in heart: and ye shall find rest unto
your souls. For my yoke is easy, and my burden is
light. (Matthew 11:25–30 KJV)

This rest is found only in the presence of God and in the stillness of the soul. Life can leave us feeling so overwhelmed physically,
mentally, and emotionally, leaving us feeling empty and dry. When
we don't take the time to spend in his presence, then we are spiritu-
ally disconnected from him. And Jesus does not want that for us at
all. He knows the importance of being in his presence. Jesus knows
the good that will come out of it for us. So he invites us to let him
calm the storms that rage deep within our soul. We are living in a
very chaotic world, and time spent in the presence of God is a must.

For in him we live, and move, and have our being;
as certain also of your own poets have said, For
we are also his offspring. (Acts 17:28 KJV)

If we want to do anything at all for Jesus, the best thing that we
can do is to sit at his feet and learn all that we can, and then he will
tell us to go share with others what he has given to us.

In his presence, we learn that in this life, there will always be
trouble. But his peace will surpass it all. We are his treasure, and he
finds his pleasure in being our great God. He is able to guide and to
provide for all his creatures, big and small. In his presence, everything
evil banished. In his presence, joy, peace, love, and happiness are
found.

You will seek me and find me when you search
for me with all your heart. (Jeremiah 29:11 KJV)

Draw nigh to God, and he will draw nigh to you.
Cleanse your hands, ye sinners; and purify your
hearts, ye double minded. (James 4:8 KJV)

Have your mind set that before you start the day, you will spend some time with your creator, the great God of the universe. If that is your heart's desire, then God will give it to you because he wants you to have that desire also. We cannot hear his voice if we are not being still. His voice is gentle and soft. It soothes our hearts and calms our fears. It silences all the other voices that are screaming lies at us. So whatever you do today, the most important thing that you will do is to spend time in the presence of God. Jesus is a loving Savior, waiting to extend his love to all that will accept him. Yes, he is indeed a friend of sinners, but he will not make you do what you don't want to do. He allows us to exercise the power of free will. It is up to you to want to be in his presence.

Sorrows

When the cup of sorrows overflows, the glory of
God will shine here below. Your friends and your
foes will question your glow as they see you shine
all in his time.

CHAPTER 3

◇◇◇

To the End

The word *end* has so many meanings to it. Today, we are going to use it in the end of time, only because I know that means the coming of Jesus is so near. For me, using the word *end* lets me know that I need to get ready for that grand event that is so soon to take place.

> But the end of all things is at hand: be ye therefore sober, and watch unto prayer. (1 Peter 4:7 KJV)

I want to be ready.

> Wherefore the rather, brethren, give diligence to make your calling and election sure: for if ye do these things, ye shall never fall. (2 Peter 1:10 KJV)

> Looking unto Jesus the author and finisher of our faith; who for the joy that was set before him endured the cross, despising the shame, and is set down at the right hand of the throne of God. (Hebrews 12:2 KJV)

I have fixed my eyes on heaven to the end.

I want to be like Enoch, who walks with God until one day, he just walked right into heaven. I want to be like Elijah, who stepped into a fiery chariot and went to heaven. But most of all, I want to be like Jesus for he is my greatest example of all. My prayers are that God will keep me faithful, bold, and courageous as I await the nearness of his soon appearance. Jesus knows that while his children would be waiting for him, some would grow faint and weary and lose their way. That is why he wants us to watch and pray at all times. Like the ten virgins in Matthews 25 (KJV), five were wise, and five were foolish. For the wise, they slept, but their lamps were trimmed and burning. When the bridegroom came, they went with him. For the foolish, they had no oil, and they were left behind.

As we live the Christian life, from day to day, we will encounter many distractions that can take our minds off Jesus. And that is the goal of the enemy—to keep us so occupied with doing even good deeds that we are not aware of the snare that he is setting for us. And thus, we too can be caught off guard and left behind. That is why we must at all time keep our lamps trimmed and burning bright. For the Master's return is nearer than it's ever been, I am determined to live for my king to the end. No turning back. No turning back. Though none go with me, still I will follow. No time to sit on the fence. You must choose today whom you will serve. Life is passing quickly, and soon, we will be standing in the presence of our holy God. And if we have not allowed him to clothed us with his robe of righteousness, then the brightness of his coming will consume us.

He is pleading for each of us to come to him today, and he will show us the way. Probation for all will end. And we must be ready. Either we are put to sleep, or Jesus will come. While we are sleeping, we are not aware of the passing of time. The next conscious thought we will have is the coming of Christ. And that, my friend, is the greatest event of all. Dear Jesus, please keep me faithful to your cause until the end. God is sealing his children and marking them as his own. I want to be in that number. I hope you do also. We are choosing our destiny each day by the way we live our lives. So please make sure that your choice of living pleases God. He will come at a time that you least expect him and at an hour that you are not aware of.

To you, that will be a surprise because you were not ready. And his coming for you will not be a pleasant one. But for all those that have made their peace with God, his coming will be a glorious event.

> And it shall be said in that day, Lo, this is our God; we have waited for him, and he will save us: this is the Lord; we have waited for him, we will be glad and rejoice in his salvation. (Isaiah 25:9 KJV)

Only those that have washed their robe white in the blood of the lamb will be able to say that. And to those that endured to the end, please make up in your mind today that you will not let nothing or no one keep you out of heaven. The enemy is a crown snatcher. Please don't let him steal your crown. We are going where he can never return to. Jesus will help you and keep you on his side if you let him. And if he is for us, who can be against us?

> And I give unto them eternal life; and they shall never perish, neither shall any man pluck them out of my hands. (John 10:28 KJV)

We must not be carried away with every wind of doctrine that blows our way. The faith we stand on must be the solid rock where nothing can shake us.

We must walk so closely by the Master's side that we can hear his gentle whisper, following him step-by-step all the way to the end. Our journey down here is long and hard. But if we stick it out, Jesus has promised that heaven will be worth it all. The trials of life will then seem so small compared to what is waiting for us over there. Life is but a drop in the bucket compared to eternity.

> For our light affliction, which is but for a moment, worketh for us a far more exceeding and eternal weight of glory. (2 Corinthians 4:17 KJV)

The joys of heaven and the splendor of its beauty will erase all memory of sin. And the greatest of all will be to see the face of Jesus. That will be heaven for me. To look upon my precious Jesus's face and have him embrace me will make me say that all the trials that life gave me was more than worth it all.

We are all living on borrowed time. The end of all things is at hand (1 Peter 4:7 KJV). Today is the day to accept Christ. He is knocking at your heart's door, waiting for you to welcome him in so that he can take your heart of stone and give you a heart of flesh. Jesus can do for you what no other can do.

> The Lord is not slack concerning his promise, as some men count slackness; but is longsuffering to us-ward, not willing that any should perish, but that all should come to repentance. (2 Peter 3:9 KJV)

This time of life will soon be over, and you will find yourself on either Christ's side or the enemy's side. The choice is yours to make. And the time to do it is now. God is looking for men and women that will stand up for him in these last days of earth's history to the end.

A Sad Heart

> My dear ones, when your heart is filled with sorrows, don't despair because the one who holds tomorrow can free you from your sorrows. Let Jesus have his way in your heart for he knows just how to clean every part. The days seem short, and the nights they do linger on. But through it all, you will find that he's been there all along to comfort and to cheer.

CHAPTER 4

<><><><><><><><><><><><><><><><><><><><><><><><><><><><><><><><><><><><>

Unshakable Faith

A faith that is firm and stands tall through the raging of any storms is a faith unshakable.

> For I say, through the grace given unto me, to every man that is among you, not to think of himself more highly than he ought to think; but to think soberly, according as God hath dealt to every man the measure of faith. (Romans 12:3 KJV)

By facing raging storms that come to us all, our faith takes a lot of beathing. And if we are not grounded firm and deep in the Savior's love, then it will not stand at all. When we choose to build our faith on Christ, the solid rock, then nothing can shake us. But if our faith is built on the things of this world, then you have nothing to stand on.

When the winds of strife blows, you will surely fall. The foundation that we need to build on is Christ Jesus. He is the rock of all ages. Our life must be wrapped up in his life. We must be so in love with him that it makes us sad to be apart from him. He is the one that is keeping us going. And we are on his heart and mind day and night. He can't wait for you and me to be reunited with him again. We should feel the same way about him. But sad to say, that is not the case with us. We are all caught up in the worldly affairs of this life, making them our priority of existence. How very sad that must make Jesus feel? He has blessed us with all things to enjoy, but the gifts are not greater than the giver.

He wants us to love and appreciate all that he has blessed us with. But he also wants more than anything for us to spend time with him, trusting him during the times that our faith may waver or be weak. If we hold onto him even in those difficult times, then we will realize that he is making diamonds out of us and perfecting our characters, allowing us to have unshakable faith. God wants only the best for his children. But sometimes, he has to show us tough love. He cannot give us all we ask for. He wants us to learn how to wait and be patient in the waiting. If we do not learn the disciplines of life, then we cannot obtain unshakable faith.

The steps that we take each day are steps that will guide us through this journey of life. We will learn what works and what doesn't work. We must make choices as we go. And the choices that we make will have a great impact on our faith, either to strengthen our faith and make it grow or to weaken our faith and make it vanish altogether. To have unshakable faith will not come easy. You will have many trials along the way. And there will be times that you will be tempted to wonder if it is really worth it all. Your faith will be tested to the max. And you will be stretched beyond reach. But if you trust God during those times, you will see that what he is doing is making you more like him. And your faith will be strong, firmed, and unshakable.

We all want life to be easy and smooth. But for the child of God, life is anything but smooth. Our faith is being built as we go. How we cope with the pressures of life and those around us is very important because they are watching us as we go through trials. When we say that we are Christians and fall apart at the least little thing that comes our way, then we are saying that our God is only able to rescue us in the good times of life. It is in the darkest days of life that our faith will grow. And the mighty name of Jesus will be honored, and you will have unshakable faith.

Don't Worry

God feeds the birds that sing the lovely songs in the spring. He lets them know that he is their heavenly king. The love he has for you and me should fill us with jubilee. So to worry and to fear is saying that he really doesn't care. His hands are open to us all when upon our knees we fall.

CHAPTER 5

<><><><><><><><><><><><><><><><><><><><><><><><><><><><><>

Learning to Exalt His Name

The precious and holy name of Jesus is to be exalted above all names. He is the only one that deserves to be exalted. He is holy, he is almighty, he is omnipresent, he is faithful, and so much more. No one else can come close to him. He is perfect in all his ways. He is precious to all that draws near to him. He is a promise-keeping, saving Savior. He is the God above all. He is all knowing. He knows the beginning from the end and all that is in between. He is the God of love. And He is the God that I exalt. He is the God that never fails. He is the great I am. He is the God of the impossible. He never sleeps, and he never slumbers. He watches over all his children night and day.

To me, that is my God whom I exalt. He guides all along the way. He knows the depth of each sinful heart, and yet he loves us just the same. He is the God of the universe. He cares for each little sparrows, and he is near to the broken in heart. He sees the tears that fall and hears the prayers of those he loves. Jesus does not have to earn exaltation. He is exalted above all. To exalt you, my Lord, is to declare to all that there is none like you. To exalt you, my king, is to give you all the glory, honor, and praise that you alone deserve. No mortals can compare to you, my eternal and loving king. No one else can do the things you do.

Man may think himself to be superior and try his best to be exalted. But all that he is comes from God. He is dust. And to dust, he will return. My Jesus is the greatest of them all. Jesus is inviting us all to come unto him and be partakers of his coronation, where every knee shall bow, and every tongue shall confess that Jesus Christ is Lord to the glory of God. He will be exalted on earth, and he will be exalted in heaven. We, mortal beings, will say holy and righteous is our God. Worship and praise belong to him forever and ever. The angels will sing, "Worthy, worthy is the lamb that sitteth upon the throne." All creatures will exalt him. When we think of all that Jesus has done, is doing, and will do, we can't help but to exalt him. He said if we don't praise him, the rocks will cry out to praise Him.

> And he answered and said unto them, I tell you
> that, if these should hold their peace, the stones
> would immediately cry out. (Luke 19:40 KJV)

As long as God gives me breath, I shall praise him. Exalting the precious name of Jesus, as Christians, we gladly give God all that he rightfully deserves. He is all worthy to receive our praise, worship, and adoration. There is no one else that can step into his shoes or even come close to it.

> But thou art holy, O thou that inhabitest the
> praises of Israel. (Psalm 22:3 KJV)

To praise him is to exalt him. Through the passing of time and the endless ages of eternity, the holy and mighty name of God will be exalted. And he doesn't need us to do it. God is God with or without us. Who he is cannot be changed. We are so privileged to be able to partake in exalting him.

I don't know about you, but I want to exalt him the rest of my life and then throughout eternity. We will never get tired of exalting the name of God.

Oh to Be Set Free

I feel trapped in this body of pain. But soon, I
shall be set free as my soul like an eagle will soar.

My eyes will behold the dawn of a new day. My body will be immortal as my feet steps on heaven's portal. Temporary is my pain as heaven soon I shall gain. My eyes, my mind, and my heart must never more depart from him whose love for me no one can tear apart.

CHAPTER 6

‹×××××××××××××××××××××××××××××××××××××××›

Endurance

Sometimes, we go through very painful and difficult situations in life. To endure is the last thing that we want to do. We just want to get whatever we are going through over with as soon as possible. But if we were to just go through trials without endurance, they would have no meaning or purpose. Endurance is not quitting when things get hard. Anyone can run a fifteen- to thirty-minute race. But running a race for life can be another story. We want life to be like the microwave food that we eat, quick and easy, without having to endure. But life is not that easy. So much stuff is coming at us from every direction. It seems like we can hardly think. The temptation to quit will be strong because it's easier to quit than to endure. But we must not give up or give in.

> Fear none of those things which thou shalt suffer: behold, the devil shall cast some of you into prison, that ye may be tried; and ye shall have tribulation ten days: be thou faithful unto death, and I will give thee a crown of life. (Revelation 2:10 KJV)

Endurance is not something that we can do on our own. Endurance is that supernatural power and strength that Jesus gives to us while running the race of life.

> Wherefore seeing we also are compassed about with so great a cloud of witnesses, let us lay aside every weight, and the sin which doth so easily beset us, and let us run with patience the race that is set before us, Looking unto Jesus the author and finisher of our faith; who for the joy that was set before him endured the cross, despising the shame, and is set down at the right hand of the throne of God. (Hebrews 12:1–2 KJV)

When we are going through the difficulties and trials of life, we must not put our focus on them. We must look to Jesus. Our eyes must not be on self. So often, when we are going through these situations of life that we have no control over, we run to the phone instead of the throne. We are looking for human empathy when we should be seeking God's sympathy. Human empathy cannot do anything for us. But God's sympathy moves his heart of love and compassion toward his hurting children. God sympathizes with us when we are going through difficulties. He sees, he hears, and he really cares. He never leaves our side. We may not see him or feel him at times, but he is there.

Even when we don't think that he is with us, he is.

> Let your conversation be without covetousness; and be content with such things as ye have: for he hath said, I will never leave thee, nor forsake thee. (Hebrews 13:5 KJV)

Endurance is what every Christian needs to have as we are coming upon the close of this earth's history. We will need to ask God to give us endurance to get through the time of trouble that is coming upon the world. These trials that we go through each and every day are preparation for the bigger ones. If we cannot endure these trials, how will we be able to endure what is ahead? So let us not murmur or complain when the cross that we are called to bear seems to be so very heavy. Let us be grateful that God is making us ready and fit for heaven.

Before the crown we wear, the cross we surely must bear. Endurance is staying true to whatever you are facing and knowing that there is no other option. Athletes that spend so much time training for the Olympics, they have to endure so much. And they are running to obtain a corruptible crown. We are all running a race.

> Know ye not that they which run in a race run all, but one receiveth the prize? So run, that ye may obtain. And every man that striveth for the mastery is temperate in all things. Now they do it to obtain a corruptible crown; but we an incorruptible. (1 Corinthians 9:24, 25 KJV)

We all need endurance to finish this race of life well. It is not how we start that really matters, but it is how we finished the course. Let us make sure that we are not running the race in vain. Let us not be so caught up with the cares of this life that we miss the purpose of that which really matters. At the end of the finish line, Jesus, our eternal prize, will be there waiting for us. And that will be the greatest prize of all. The key to endurance is not looking to self, but to Jesus. He will give us just what we need and when we need it. The training that we are going through now is very intense. And sometimes, we are tempted to just quit. But remember that we are not alone in this race. God goes before us. And he guides us along the way. He will never leave us to run this race alone. He measures out the amount of trials that you and I are to go through. And he will never allow more to come to us than we can bear.

God is not out to crush us beneath the burdens of life. We are living in the time of the great controversy. And we have an enemy that is trying his best to destroy us. We are caught up in this battle that is for the human soul. God is doing all that he can to keep us on his side. And to do so, he is preparing us for this battle. Each and every day and all throughout the day, we are in constant warfare. We must not quit or retrieve. We must endure to the end. The enemy is a defeated foe. His days are number, and he knows it. You and I must know that God loves us too much to leave us. He tells us in his holy word that we can do all things through him (Philippians 4:13 KJV). We are almost home now. The race is almost over. Eternity is almost in view. I can almost hear my Jesus calling my name, telling me to endure. The conflict of sin is almost over. And the victory already is won. Christ's coming is near, even at the door. To endure to the end will be the greatest test of all.

We can do it if we hold onto Jesus. He promised never to let us go. And nothing can take us out of his hands. So my dear ones, whatever you are going through today, give it to Jesus. He already sees how you are struggling beneath the cares of life. He said that his grace is enough to see you through it all (2 Corinthians 12:9 KJV). He will give you the courage, strength, and endurance that he knows you will need to get you through it.

Desires That Kills

Sin is not a game that you should entertain. All have complained that sin really does stain. But to call on God is never in vain. The enemy of our souls has only one goal, and that is to turn our bodies into charcoal. Ashes to ashes, the preacher will say of you and me someday. But God who loves us all will keep us from the fall when upon him we must call.

CHAPTER 7

<><><><><><><><><><><><><><><><><><><><><><><><><><><><><><><><>

Learning to Hear God's Voice

When we are rushing through life at a high speed and never stopping to take time to enjoy all the beautiful things that God has placed in our path to enjoy, then we cannot hear his voice. God speaks to us in many ways. And nature is one of those ways that God uses to communicate to those that choose to listen. God can speak through people. Sometimes, he also speaks through his word, and most of all, God speaks through his Holy Spirit. He speaks to us in the stillness of the soul. Psalm 46:10 (KJV) says, "Be still, and know that I am God: I will be exalted among the heathen, I will be exalted in the earth." Jesus is calling us apart from the cares of life that rob us from spending time with him. He knows that life can be very overwhelming at times and that we are going to need to lean on him for comfort, strength, and support. If the enemy can keep us distracted with all kinds of things, then we are more likely to fall prey to his traps.

Spending time in the presence of God is a must. There, we can hear him speak to us clearly. And nothing should come between your soul and your Savior. Jesus can calm the raging storms in our lives. He speaks peace, and even the winds obey. His voice makes the difference like no other voice can. He wants us to experience his peace at all times. He whispers ever so gently to us. How his ways are so much better than the cares, worries, fears, and anxiety that can steal our peace and joy. Jesus wants us to rest in him from burdens that we are carrying each day. Jesus sees and knows how we are struggling just to keep our heads afloat, trying to swim through the waves of life.

> Come unto me, all ye that labour and are heavy laden, and I will give you rest. Take my yoke upon you, and learn of me; for I am meek and lowly in heart: and ye shall find rest unto your souls. For my yoke is easy, and my burden is light. (Matthew 11:28–30 KJV)

Before we get out of bed in the morning and the last thing at night, we should be spending time talking to God and listening to the still small voice of the Master speaking to us. When we stop to listen to God's voice, then we can hear him give us directions that will be our guide through this life. If we are truly seeking him, we will find him already there waiting for us. To hear God's voice, one must be in tune. He speaks when we are still and meditating on his word. Jesus knows that we are humans. He knows just how frail his children are. He knows and sees the danger that lays ahead of us. We can't see it, but he can. Jesus knows that the plans of the enemy is to distract us from spending time with him. And thus, we will live in a life of constant fear and being totally robed of the joy, peace, and happiness that the Master has in store for all those that truly are seeking him. He wants us to learn to abide in him. Outside of him are chaos and confusion. But when we are making the necessary time to be with him, he can walk with us and talk with us. And what a sweet communion that will be as we walk together, the Lord and us. Jesus is like the mother hen that gathers her baby chicks under her wings to keep them safe from harm.

> He shall cover thee with his feathers, and under his wings shalt thou trust: his truth shall be thy shield and buckler. (Psalm 91:4 KJV)

God is not trying to keep us away from him. He wants only what is best for his children. God does not want us to be tied down with all that we are facing. Time with him must not be neglected. When we make the time to spend with our dear Lord, then we can face anything. Jesus tells us that in this world, we will have trouble, but we are not to let trouble overwhelm us. If we are resting in him, then we will hear his voice of peace, assuring us that he is with us all the way to the end. It is when we are dwelling in his peace that he can speak peace to us. It soothes our troubled mind. And he assures us that he is in full control of it all.

As long as we choose to stay in his presence, his love will bind us to him. And once we are locked safe and secure in his circle of love, nothing or no one can pluck us out of his care.

> What shall we then say to these things? If God be for us, who can be against us? He that spared not his own Son, but delivered him up for us all, how shall he not with him also freely give us all things? Who shall lay any thing to the charge of God's elect? It is God that justifieth. Who is he that condemneth? It is Christ that died, yea rather, that is risen again, who is even at the right hand of God, who also maketh intercession for us. Who shall separate us from the love of Christ? shall tribulation, or distress, or persecution, or famine, or nakedness, or peril, or sword? As it is written, For thy sake we are killed all the day long; we are accounted as sheep for the slaughter. Nay, in all these things we are more than conquerors through him that loved us. For I am persuaded, that neither death, nor life, nor angels, nor principalities, nor powers, nor things present, nor things to come, Nor height, nor depth, nor any other creature, shall be able to separate us from the love of God, which is in Christ Jesus our Lord. (Romans 8:31–39 KJV)

As the world rushes on and the demands for us to perform tasks can be so very overwhelming that at the end of the day, we are so overly exhausted and frustrated that we jump into our beds to get a few hours of sleep, only to do it all over again, that is not the life that Jesus has for his children. He is calling us to come apart with him before we fall apart from the cares of life.

He wants us to make him the center of our lives so that he can be the one to guide us along the way with his kind and gentle words. He whispers to us his peace when we are restless and afraid. His peace to us is like no other.

> Peace I leave with you, my peace I give unto you:
> not as the world giveth, give I unto you. Let not
> your heart be troubled, neither let it be afraid.
> (John 14:27 KJV)

When we are in tune with the voice of Jesus, we will be able to detect his voice above the loudest crowds. He said, "My sheep hear my voice, and they follow me" (John 10:27 KJV). When we choose to set time aside for God, there are multitudes of blessings that follow.

In this world, you will have chaos, fear, and anxiety that steals our peace. Jesus loves us so very much that it hurts him to see us struggle when all we have to do is come to him. He stands with open arms to welcome his wayward children into his rest. Today, if you feel that your life is fallen apart, and you don't know what to do about it, remember that Jesus is the answer to all of life's troubles. When you invite him into your life, you will learn to hear his voice. You will not benefit by someone else's experience with Jesus. You have to experience him for yourself. He is a personal God. Only you can make the choice to have a personal relationship with the Creator of the universe.

He is not a God that is faraway. He is very near. He is a big God, who rules his mighty universe, yet he is small enough to live within each heart that welcomes him in. He wants us to hear his voice and be obedient to all that he bids us to do. Today, you can start your own personal relationship with the great God of heaven. Let him speak to you, and you will hear his voice for yourself.

Standing on the Rock

To one and to all, I'm here to say choose God's way, and don't go astray. Please stop today to pray so you don't lose your way. There is coming a day when God will repay the deeds of this mortal clay. But you need not fear when you know that God is near, ready to comfort and ready to cheer. So you see, his name you must always declare. He is our rock, and we are his flock.

CHAPTER 8

~~~~~~

Learning to Wait on God

We are living in a very fast track of life, where no one wants to hear the word *wait*. Life is at a high speed, and if you can't run with it, you will get run over or be left behind. We start to complain if we have to wait in line or on the phone. We complain when the microwave oven takes too long. All of this is because life is at a high speed. And when it comes for us to be waiting on God, we want it to be on our turn. But that is not how it works. God's timing is not our timing. He teaches us to wait in order to teach us patience. It is in the waiting period that he can do for us what no one else can do.

Waiting is a skill that can only be developed when you allow Jesus to be your peace. For you see if you are not resting in his love divine, then you will be overwhelmed by your situations. Waiting could be very frustrating. And if you don't have God's peace abiding in you, then waiting for you will be a time of torture. The Bible has a lot to say about waiting.

> I waited patiently for the Lord; and he inclined unto me, and heard my cry. (Psalm 40:1 KJV)

> Wait on the Lord: be of good courage, and he shall strengthen thine heart: wait, I say, on the Lord. (Psalm 27:14 KJV)

> I wait for the Lord, my soul doth wait, and in his
> word do I hope. (Psalm 130:5 KJV)

At some point or another, each of us will have to learn how to wait. We cannot do it on our own.

> I am the vine, ye are the branches: He that abideth in me, and I in him, the same bringeth forth much fruit: for without me ye can do nothing. (John 15:5 KJV)

We are not to think that we know more than God. When we have that attitude, then we will miss out on the best that life has to offer us. And that is learning to wait on God.

When we rush through life, we miss opportunities that God can use to be a blessing to someone. Life is so much calmer when it is at a slow pace. We meet friends along the way, and we learn as we go how to wait on God. When we are hasty, it will show in every area of our life. Learning to wait on God can be a great blessing if we allow it to be. As adults, we pass on the same impatient character to our children. Believe it or not, they are learning from us, both the good and the bad. So let us make sure that whatever we are teaching others, it is pleasing to God. He wants us all to learn to wait on him. When we do that, then God can bless us with what he sees that we need, not what we want. When we can wait, and we have peace while waiting, that is a gift that only God can give. When you think about it, we are the ones that loses out when we choose not to wait.

God's ways of doing things is so much better. We must ask him to please help us to learn to wait on him. And he will do just that. He said that he knows the plan that he has for our life, plans to prosper us and not to harm us (Jeremiah 29:11 KJV). And when God tells us to wait on him, that means that he has something better for us than what we can get on our own. When we learn to put God first in all that we do and say, then waiting on him will come much easier. If we don't have a relationship with God, then we will find it hard to obey him. He sees what we don't see. And he knows what we don't know.

God sees the big picture, while we see only a dot. Sometimes, we ask for things that will harm us or harm someone else. We don't see the danger in what we ask for, but God does. Or sometimes, it's just selfish motives that we have. We think that we must have everything that our hearts desire. And we must have it now. That is what the world tells us.

> For as the heavens are higher than the earth, so are my ways higher than your ways, and my thoughts than your thoughts. (Isaiah 55:9 KJV)

We are influencing people every day in one way or the other. Waiting can also be a testimony. When those around us know how we go through our trials and how we wait on God to see us through them, their life can also be changed. Waiting on God does not mean that he is going to perfect our life and make everything go smooth. Waiting on God is so we can have the assurance that his peace and presence are with us always even if he chooses not to change our circumstances.

Just about everything in life requires us to wait, it will make us either better or bitter. Waiting is a part of life. We wait to be born, and we wait to die. And all the rushing and hastiness that we do will not change the fact that we still have to wait for something or someone. Waiting should not be wasted. It should be a time well spent. When we are waiting on God to do his will for us, then we are to praise him in that waiting period and serve others as we wait. Then God will be please with us. We have taken the attention off us and placed it on others. Sometimes, we think that we are the only one with problems and that our issues are the only ones that really matters.

We are living in a world of hurting and suffering people. Our God sees it all. As we wait for him to come and end it all, we must patiently endure the cross before the crown. There are hope, joy, peace, and eternal life at the end of the waiting process. So you see, my dear ones, God always knows just what he is doing. (Always) our waiting and suffering are not in vain. Today, I waited on the phone for two hours with a company that I really needed to get in contact with. That waiting was surely in vain but not when we wait on the Lord. Great is our reward.

No matter how long the wait may be, remember that we can trust our God. He will always come through for us. He is never late, and he is never early. But he is always on time. When God gives us an assignment on waiting, that is because he wants to give us more than what we ask him for. God doesn't just do things because he can do them. He has a purpose and a plan for all that he does. He will not waste your time of waiting but greatly reward you if you are patiently waiting on him and praising him as you wait. When God gets the glory for all that we endure, then he knows that he can trust us with our waiting assignment.

The Colors of the Rainbow

You may be black, or you may be white, but God has made you just right. If you are brown, please don't frown. Soon, God will give you a golden crown. We are made of many colors that help us to discover that Christ has made us through his power. We are each unique. But it doesn't mean that we are weak. To love the colors that you meet will make you humble, meek, and sweet.

CHAPTER 9

<><><><><><><><><><><><><><><><><><><><><><><><><><><><><><><>

When It Seems Like God Is Silent

There comes a time in each of our lives when we think that God is not listening, or he just doesn't care. It seems like no matter how much we pray, God is still silent, but I've learned that his silence does not mean he is absent.

> God is our refuge and strength, a very present help in trouble. (Psalm 46:1 KJV)

The enemy of our souls wants us to believe that our God is not a God that we can trust. Please don't believe his lies. Our God loves us all with an everlasting love. And we can trust him in the good times as well as the bad times. When you are having thoughts of doubt, and your mind is full of questions, please take them to God. He will assure you that he is in full control and that all you need to do is to trust him. When we allow our fears to be bigger than our faith, that is because we have taken our eyes off Jesus. We must look back at what he has done for us in the past and believe that he can do it again for us in the present as well as in the future.

When we are overcome by feelings, then we have opened the door for the enemy to come into our lives and destroy us. As Christians, we live by faith, not by feelings or fear. We must spend much time in the Holy Word of God and on our knees, seeking his guidance and help daily. If we don't do that, then we will be easy prey to those that are out to devour us.

> Watch and pray, that ye enter not into temptation: the spirit indeed is willing, but the flesh is weak. (Matthew 26:41 KJV)

> Put on the whole armour of God, that ye may be able to stand against the wiles of the devil. (Ephesians 6:11 KJV)

Our God may be silent at times, but please know that he is never absent.

> Let your conversation be without covetousness; and be content with such things as ye have: for he hath said, I will never leave thee, nor forsake thee. (Hebrews 13:5 KJV)

> Let, I pray thee, thy merciful kindness be for my comfort, according to thy word unto thy servant. (Psalm 119:76 KJV)

What God did for us yesterday, he is well able to do it again for us today and tomorrow, God willing. We must not lose hope and then give up.

Giving up, for the Christians, is not an option. We have nowhere else to go. Jesus is our only hope. In each of our lives, there will be dark days and hard times that will fill us with questions and leave us with doubts, which will be the beginning of a life that will spin us into a downward position, leading us further and further away from God, the only one that can and wants to help us. God's silence is his assurance that he really is with us, and we must believe deep in our hearts that he knows just what he is doing. Our faith in him will be the key to lead us out of whatever situations that we are facing. We must learn how to turn our eyes upon Jesus, and the things of earth will grow strangely dim, in the light of his glory and grace (Hymn #290 in SDA Church hymnal). We are living in a world full of sin. The results, therefore, are chaos, fear, worries, and anxiety, leaving us feeling trap in the snare of the enemy. Then we think that life is hopeless. Those thoughts are not of God. Those are lies of the father of lies.

> For I know the thoughts that I think toward you,
> saith the Lord, thoughts of peace, and not of evil,
> to give you an expected end. (Jeremiah 29:11 KJV)

Yes, there will be times in our lives that the rain of trouble will fall, and trials will seem to have no end. And you cannot see the sunlight in view. Those days will be where your faith will be tested to the max. But if you choose to still trust God during those times, you will be greatly rewarded. And the precious name of our Lord Jesus Christ will be honored. And that, my friend, is what it is all about. We must not only expect good from the hands of God. Although he doesn't send the bad stuff that comes to us, he allows it so that he can work it out for his glory and our good. And he does not allow it because he is God, and he can do anything. While that is true, he allows trials and troubles to come to us to refine us and to make us better fit for his kingdom. Trials are to make us more like our dear Jesus. He disciplines and corrects those he loves, if our earthly parents can discipline us, and sometimes, they do it harshly, leaving us not only bruised but also broken in spirit. Our loving heavenly Father does not discipline us for the sake of seeing us suffer. He does it out of love for us. No discipline seems pleasant at the time, but painful.

> Now no chastening for the present seemeth to
> be joyous, but grievous: nevertheless afterward
> it yieldeth the peaceable fruit of righteousness
> unto them which are exercised thereby. (Hebrews
> 12:11 NIV)

Not only does God discipline us, but also he tenderly and lovingly leads us along the way, always wanting only what is best for each of his children. When we are experiencing dry seasons in our lives, and it seems like God is silent, that is because he is our teacher, and we are taking a test. The teacher is always silent during test time. We are to trust God even when we can't trace him. We may not understand or know all that is going on in our lives or know the reason why we are going through what we are going through when one is dealing with chronic pain, and the light at the end of the tunnel is hard to see, but that is when we are to say, "Father God, I don't know what you are doing or where you are taking me, but I choose to trust you." That is the case with me. I have severe back pain. And there are days when the pain just doesn't stop. It goes from bad to worse. But it is in those dark and painful times that I am drawn so much closer to my dear Savior.

Knowing that he has suffered so much more than that for me, there are a lot of things that I am limited to do, but I am praising God for all that I can still do. And praising him in the midst of the storms is my greatest joy. At times, the situation does not change. But the peace that I get out of praising him in my pain is so rewarding.

We don't need to understand. We just need to hold God's hand. One day, if he chooses, he will explain life to us. But if he doesn't, that too is okay because he is God, and we are not. He is gently leading us in the path that we should go. It may very well be a path of much pain, sorrows, grief, and suffering, but we can still trust him to lead, guide, and provide. He knows the path that is best for us, and he will guide us with his eyes and uphold us with his mighty right hand. We can close our eyes, and as long as we are allowing God to guide us, we don't need to fear at all. Oftentimes, we fear what we cannot see or what we don't have control over. But when we learn to let go and let God be God in our life, things will be much easier for us.

As we learn to trust him and let him lead the way, we are in good hands. We are in the hands of Jesus. Our future is safe and secure, knowing that God has only good in store for his children. Our job is to stay faithful, meek, and humble, never questioning the plans of our great creator, only trusting him. We are to continue in doing good to those around us so that they can see God's light shining in us. Even when we think that God is being silence, our light in him must never grow dimmed. He is not sitting in heaven doing nothing. God is seeing it all, and he is taking note of all that is going on with his children. Let us not become weary and discouraged because we may not, at the time, be hearing from God.

It's like the poem "Footprints in the Sand" when we are going through hard and painful times, and we can't seem to see God working or hear him speaking. That is because he is carrying us through those times.

> But when he saw the wind boisterous, he was afraid; and beginning to sink, he cried, saying, Lord, save me. (Matthew 14:30 KJV)

Sometimes, you may feel like you are drowning beneath the waves of life, and all hope seems to be lost. But, my friend, I promise you that if you can hold on, no matter what, God will turn your trials into triumph, your test into a testimony, and your mess into a message for him. God did not promise us that every time we seek him that he would answer our every beckon calls. Although he hears all of our prayers and does answer them in the way that he knows is best for us, he does not act like a genie in a lamp, just waiting to grant our wishes.

He is the great God of the universe that wants to give us so much more than just to meet our physical need. He wants us to experience the whole package that comes with being a human. That is body, soul, and mind. And God knows each area we are struggling in.

> Beloved, I wish above all things that thou mayest prosper and be in health, even as thy soul prospereth. (3 John 1:2 KJV)

While we are trying to be healthy and prosperous, we are neglecting the most important thing. And that is to have a deep relationship with our great God. Sometimes, suffering can be blessings in disguise. For the Christians, they can draw nearer to God in their time of suffering. For those that doesn't know God, suffering can make them want to know God or can push them further away. But for the Christians, even in the midst of it all, we can have peace while we are going through our trials. So the next time you are tempted to think that God is being silent in the midst of your chaos, please think again. That is the time that he is the closest to you. Don't allow anything or anyone to shake your faith and cause you to have doubt about the great God of love. He gave his all for you and me. And surely, he will not leave us now.

> Being confident of this very thing, that he which hath begun a good work in you will perform it until the day of Jesus Christ. (Philippians 1:6 KJV)

God has invested far too much in you and me to leave us now. And remember that God's silence is not that he's absent.

God Is Always Near

> The night of sorrows will soon be over as we await a brighter tomorrow. To enjoy today will clearly say that God is leading all the way. He listens to us as we stop to pray, and gently, he comforts along the way. Though the nights can be long, God will always stick around. I have a friend that loves me to the end. I truly recommend that you on him can depend.

CHAPTER 10

<><><><><><><><><><><><><><><><><><><><><><><><><><><><><><>

The Uncertainties of Life

We think that we have life all figured out. And we make our plans to do this, that, and the other. But our life is not our own. We are so very fragile.

> Whereas ye know not what shall be on the morrow. For what is your life? It is even a vapour, that appeareth for a little time, and then vanisheth away. (James 4:14 KJV)

We are just passing through this land on our way to a better land. God, our Father, is telling us that we are not to get comfortable in a strange land and not to give all our time and energy to obtain worldly possessions. We are living in some very uncertain times. And we don't just want to live for the here and now. We want to live our lives with eternity, always in mind as things can change drastically and suddenly. And if we have made preparation for this world only, then we will miss out on what really matters. And that is eternal life with Jesus. When we aim for all that this life can give us, we hold it loosely in our hands. It is like trying to hold onto the wind. When we die and leave our wealth to someone else. They will come along and reap your harvest, all your hard work of labor, and toiling will be in vain.

This life is very uncertain. And tomorrow is not promise to any of us. God knows that we need to work and be occupied till he comes, but he does not want man to be enslaved by his earthly possessions. We must put God first at all times in our lives. It is God that gives us health to get wealth. God is not against us having wealth. He does not want the wealth to have us. We are stewards to all that he has blessed us with. All that we have belongs to him. We are to live our lives as though each day could be our last. God wants us to be wise with whatever he has blessed us with. We are to invest in souls for eternity, not to build bigger houses and buy more and more earthly toys. People are dying all around us every day. Many are going to a Christless grave while we are occupied with obtaining more and more of this life. At the end of it all, we will stand before God with nothing. Only our transformed character and the souls of those that we have led to Christ, "Only one life, and then it is passed. Only what we do for Christ will last" (C.T. Studd). When we live a life of full service to God, then we are complete. It is only then that we can stand before God with a clear conscience.

Heaven will be full of the many precious souls. They will be there because we have taken the time to invest in them. The gold and silver that we accumulate down here will be of no value up there. God is interested in precious souls, and we should be also. Time is short, and death is sure. When lifework on earth is done, and a golden crown you won, then you will see that it was truly worthy it all.

Even though we are living in uncertain times, we can still see people living as though the world will never end. You and I must not fall into that category. We are Christians, and as Christians, we are longing for the return of our dear Lord Jesus, which can't be much longer now. We can go to bed tonight, and that could be the end of us for this life. We don't know when we will take our last breath or the trumpet will sound, and the next face we see will be Jesus. That could all take place in a moment. We must all be prepared for the uncertainties of life.

Holding On

My heart is in heaven. My body is on earth. And
I am awaiting my final new birth. When soon I
shall be set free from the cares of life that leave
me wounded and scared, I do declare that my
Master is always so near.

CHAPTER 11

<><><><><><><><><><><><><><><><><><><><><><><><><><><><><><><>

Radical Living

When I hear the word radical, I think of an extreme person. But if we could be radical for Jesus, that would be great. We would be Christians on fire. And then we could turn the world upside down, being bold, courageous, and strong for Jesus. I believe that God is looking for such people. He wants us to be radical for him because the days that we are living in are days leading up to the end. And more than ever, we must be on fire for him. When we were living the worldly life, some of us were very radical. So now, all we have to do is be more radical for Jesus. We must be willing to do whatever it takes to serve the Lord and be willing to go anywhere he leads us. He will take us out of our comfort zone and place us in some very uncomfortable situations so that we will learn the value of serving others. Radical living is the only way to go for Jesus. We must go all the way out on the limb, taking risks, learning, and trusting only in the guidance of our God, choosing to stay on his side no matter what.

And when we have made that choice to go all the way with Jesus, then he will honor us in ways that we cannot imagine. Radical living is what we are called to do as Christians. We are supposed to have a mindset on doing the right thing. Our minds must be transformed, changed to the ways of God and not of the world. We must not say that we are Christians only, but our lives should be a strong testimony of what we profess. We cannot say that we are living a radical Christian life only in words. Our actions speak louder than words. Christ Jesus is not looking for Christians only in words but in both action and words. He is calling us to be the fireball that the world needs in these last days. We are surrounded by witnesses of all kind. All heaven is watching us, all those we come in contact with are watching us, and all the fallen world are watching us. All of heaven is cheering us on, and those we see every day are waiting for us to mess up so that they can ridicule us. As the evil-fallen ones see us. They are trying to make us like them, fallen and without hope, but praise God for his precious gift, our Lord Jesus, who has paid the debt in full. And because of what Jesus did, we have hope and eternal life. And God is waiting to fill us up with his power that we can have what it takes to live radical. Without the empowering of the Holy Spirit, we cannot live the Christian radical life.

The Face of Jesus

O to look upon your face when at last I've run this race, trusting only in your grace and knowing that one day we shall soon embrace. When I look up into space, it tells me that you could never be replaced.

CHAPTER 12

<><><><><><><><><><><><><><><><><><><><><><><><><><><><>

The God of the Impossible

Behold, I am the Lord, the God of all flesh: is
there any thing too hard for me?
                                        —Jeremiah 32:27 (KJV)

We are living in a world where everyone thinks themself to be self-suf-
ficient. No one feels like they need help, especially divine help. But
there will always be a brick wall waiting for us to run into it. We are
created creatures. Only our great creator knows it all. We will forever
and always need his help. For some of us, we don't have to fall too far
to realize that we need help in the worst kind of way. For others that
are so full of themselves, that divine help will come to them when
they have emptied their heart of self. We are limited creatures. God,
our creator, has made us that way. We are growing and learning, not
just in time on earth but throughout the endless ages of eternity. We
don't want to hear that there are things that we cannot do. We, as
human, want to say that we can do it all. And when we fail at impossible tasks, we fall apart because we don't know how to handle failure.
God is always ready to help us. He is the God that can do it all.

He raised the dead, he heals the sick, he opens the eyes of the
blind, he opens the ears of the deaf, and he fed the multitude with
just two fishes and five loaves of breads. So you see, my friend, there
is nothing impossible for God. Your problems and mine are nothing
for him. He wants to help us. And he wants us to feel comfortable

coming to him for help. We, as Christians, know that we can come to our great creator, redeemer, sustainer, and friend for anything and at any time. We don't have to wait until we are in an impossible situation.

God wants to have a relationship with each of us. We should not just seek his giving hands or know him for what he can give us while he is the God of the impossible.

> But thou art holy, O thou that inhabits the praise
> of Israel. (Psalms 22:3 KJV)

Our God is not waiting to grant us wishes but to meet our every need. He said if we call out to him, he is ready to do the impossible for us.

Feeling Blue

> Life can leave us sometimes wondering about so many things. But when you find yourself doubting, just start shouting, and when you don't have a clue, please know that God hears you. So there is no need to feel blue because our God is always true. Your strength in him he will renew as he carries you through.

CHAPTER 13

<><><><><><><><><><><><><><><><><><><><><><><><><><><><><><><><><><><>

In the Furnace of Affliction

For the Christians, the word furnace is not anything new. We are always in the fiery furnace. We do not like the word *affliction* because we know that it has suffering attached to it.

> Yea, and all that will live godly in Christ Jesus
> shall suffer persecution. (2 Timothy 3:12 KJV)

Persecution comes in many forms. It could be with someone trying to take your life for your faith. Or it could also come to us with our health, as it is for so many of us. But the outcome is the same. We are to stay faithful no matter what.

When God allows us to go through persecution, he is making us fit and ready for the atmosphere of heaven. Without going through persecution, we will not take the Christian life seriously. And the view of the cross will be diminished. All the suffering that our dear Savior did for us will be less appreciated if we ourselves don't experience some kind of suffering.

> Blessed are those who are persecuted because
> of righteousness, for theirs is the kingdom of
> heaven. (Matthew 5:10 NIV)

If you are not going the same way of the world, you will be afflicted and persecuted. When we choose to follow Christ and go against the current, then we will be faced with much affliction. And sometimes, we think that it will happen only to those afar off. But sometimes, the greatest affliction and persecution take place within your own families. They will be the ones to inflict the hardest blows. And because we love them so much, it will hurt us the most. But we are to stay true and faithful to the cause of Christ no matter what befalls us.

> Fear none of those things which thou shalt suffer: behold, the devil shall cast some of you into prison, that ye may be tried; and ye shall have tribulation ten days: be thou faithful unto death, and I will give thee a crown of life. (Revelation 2:10 KJV)

Affliction is a word that perhaps we try to avoid. But when we look at it in the light of what Jesus went through for us, we will see that no one has suffered what Christ suffered for the sake of the human race.

Then we will see that what we are going through, however great and painful it may be, it will be light affliction. Jesus will forever and ever bear the scars of the price of sin. You and I may have scars that we have as we pass through this life, but when we see Jesus, they will all be a thing of the past.

> And one shall say unto him, What are these wounds in thine hands? Then he shall answer, Those with which I was wounded in the house of my friends. (Zachariah 13:6 KJV)

Afflictions for the believers is a way of keeping us close to our dear Jesus and reminding us that after this life is all over, we shall spend eternity with the one who loves us so much. And then we will realize that it was worth it all. Just being in the presence of our holy

God and viewing the splendors of heaven, we will see that our trials and afflictions indeed we're more than worth it all. So please don't get discouraged or dismayed when you are going through afflictions. They will do one of two things for you, draw you closer to God, or take you further away from him. It's up to you what you allow it to do. Affliction is not a word that we, as Christians, should shun. We must face it with courage, knowing that affliction produces much fruits. And if we are not bearing fruits, then we are not making progress for the kingdom of God. And God want's all his Christian children to bear fruits. So he allows us to be pruned. And being pruned is no fun, which is the same as being afflicted.

At the time, we may not like it, but if we endure it to the end, then we will see the harvest of it. As long as we are being afflicted, that means that we are still living in a world of sin. But a glad and glorious day is soon to come, where all that we are passing through now will never be even a memory. Afflictions will not last long. But Jesus and all of heaven will last without end. So whatever afflictions you may be passing through at the moment, please hold on to the strong hand of Jesus, and know that he will not let you go until you are safe in his harbor.

> For his anger endureth but a moment; in his favour is life: weeping may endure for a night, but joy cometh in the morning. (Psalms 30:5 KJV)

So don't be afraid of affliction. Count it as joy for your Lord.

Open Eyes

> Lord, please open my eyes that I may see that greater is you that is within me. I need not fear the terror or snare that seems to draw ever so near. My heart is glad because you are not mad. Your love for me has set me free so I can live a life of joy and glee.

CHAPTER 14

<><><><><><><><><><><><><><><><><><><><><><><><><><><><><><><><><>

The Attitude of Gratitude

When we learn to have an attitude of being grateful for all that comes our way, then we send confusion to the enemy camp. We know that all good things come from God, but we also know that God allows us to experience painful things at times for reason known only to him. The evil ones take advantage of the opportunities when they can throw their fiery darts at us, hoping to knock down for good. But instead, those fiery darts knock us to our knees, where we are strengthened and encouraged. And instead of complaining, we can have the attitude of always being grateful even in the midst of all that is coming after us. We can still say thank you, Jesus, and when we learn how to say thank you, and truly mean it, in the very midst of our pain and suffering, God is glorified. And we have shifted the attention off ourself and onto God where it really belongs. Being grateful, and having a positive attitude on life, is very helpful and hopeful for the Christians because we know that these things that we are going through are only temporal. We can't imagine all that is awaiting us at the end of this journey we call life. We live each day in anticipation of the day when we will see Jesus face-to-face. But while we are waiting to see him, we must go through some hard times. And staying on the grateful side of life even when it hurts will be rewarding in the end.

It is very hard to be thankful, and grateful, when life is knocking us down with one blow after another. We cannot be in an attitude of gratitude without the love of God dwelling in us.

> In every thing give thanks: for this is the will of God in Christ Jesus concerning you. (1 Thessalonians 5:18 KJV)

God can give us what we need to stay in the attitude of gratitude. And only by his grace and mercy will he be able to carry us through the trials of this life. Sometimes, there is so much going on that we focus only on the bad and not the good. And we forget that there is good in everything if we look for it. There is good in pain. We can be thankful that we are able to feel the pain. When we focus only on the bad situations of life, then that becomes our life. And instead of being grateful, we will become grumblers and complainers.

We are the ones to choose which way we will go when life is knocking us down and pressing us between the rock and the hard place. Jesus wants us to keep our focus on him. And the things of earth will strangely grow dim in the light of his glory and grace (Hymn #290 in SDA Church Hymnal). We are to be happy and grateful Christians. That will take time and practice. But if we can start small, then we soon will realize that we are being grateful for things that we would normally complain about. God is moved by our grateful attitude. But we make him sad when all we do is complain. So today if you are in any situation that is testing your faith, and you want to murmur and complain, please have the attitude of gratitude instead. You will feel much better. And God will be glorified for your suffering.

Sickness and Health

> Dear Jesus, should you choose to heal me, I'll be very grateful. And if you choose to make me whole, body and soul, which I know is your gold, I am content to wait until I enter those pearly gates. And my heart will be free from all that troubles me.

CHAPTER 15

<><><><><><><><><><><><><><><><><><><><><><><><><><><><><><><><><><><>

Knowing Your Worth and Value

Sometimes, when life beats us up so bad, and it seems to leave us thinking that we have no worth or value to ourself or to others, we must always remember that to God, we are the most precious things on this earth. In his sight, we will never lose our value. Sin has a way of robbing us of that which is precious to us. And that is our soul. But when we choose to totally surrender our life to God, sin cannot touch that which we have given to God.

> And I give unto them eternal life; and they shall never perish, neither shall any man pluck them out of my hands. (John 10:28 KJV)

When we are feeling worthless and useless, that is not the plans of God for our life.

> For I know the thoughts that I think toward you, saith the Lord, thoughts of peace, and not of evil, to give you an expected end. (Jeremiah 29:11 KJV)

When we have low self-esteem and are in a constant state of depression, that is when the enemy comes in like a flood to steel our joy, peace, and happiness.

Jesus said that he will not allow the enemy to overtake us. Our God is in full control. We are to cry out to him when we are being tempted in any way. We must not believe the lies of the enemy. We are greatly beloved by our heavenly Father. He loves us so very much that he gives us his only dear son, our Lord Jesus, to save us. When you are feeling down and out, that is the time for you to check your thinking and tell yourself that God loves you, and you are very special to him. Our thought life is so very important. We must think about what we are thinking about because stinking thinking can lead you down the path of no return. Philippians 4:8 (KJV) says, "Finally, brethren, whatsoever things are true, whatsoever things are honest, whatsoever things are just, whatsoever things are pure, whatsoever things are lovely, whatsoever things are of good report; if there be any virtue, and if there be any praise, think on these things." In other words, think only on good things. We do not have to meditate on the garbage that comes our way all the time.

We can choose to replace it with positive thoughts. Everything that takes place in our life starts in the mind. That is why we must daily spend time in the Word of God, asking him to replace those bad thoughts with his promises. The next time that the enemy comes to you with his lies and trying to devalue you, please remember that if you were the only one on earth, Jesus would have still given his life for you. Each and every one of us are so very special to Jesus. We are so valuable to him that all the silver and all the gold couldn't purchase us. Instead, he bought us with all that he had. And that, my friend, was his precious, precious blood. Nothing else would do.

Don't look to the world for worth. It can't give it to you. Having a sense of worthlessness is just what the enemy wants you to have. But God wants you to be free from all negative thinking.

> For who hath known the mind of the Lord, that he may instruct him? but we have the mind of Christ (1 Corinthians 2:16 KJV).

> And be not conformed to this world: but be ye transformed by the renewing of your mind, that

ye may prove what is that good, and acceptable,
and perfect, will of God. (Romans 12:2)

He tells us that we are not to conform to the pattern of this
world but be transformed by the renewing of your mind. So from
this moment on, tell yourself that you are very valuable, not because
of what you did but because of what Jesus did. For the worth of my
soul, he made me whole.

Your Plans for My Life

Please show me your plans for my life today so
that I can please you in every way. To live a life
of service is to live a life for you. And as I give to
others, you will give to me. In some small way I
pray, please use me today.

CHAPTER 16

<<<<<<<<<<<<<<<<<<<<<<<<<<<<<<<<<<<<<<<<<<<<<<<<<<<>

We Are Living in a Time of Trouble

The Bible speaks of a time of trouble that is coming upon the whole world like never before. We are in those times now. Today, you don't have to go far to see trouble. It is everywhere. We are perplexed on every side, living in constant fear because of all that is going on around us. If there is ever a time that we need to be calling on the name of the Lord, it is now out of desperation. People are doing all kind of evil and committing so much crime and violence. We are living and dwelling in a grand and awful time. These are the days that we must turn our eyes upon Jesus and look upon him, and the things of this earth will grow strangely dim in the light of his glory and grace. When we cry out to God in the midst of our trouble, he hears us and allows us to enter into his peace. Sometimes, because of all that is going on around us, we can feel a little overwhelmed by it all and feel like we are losing grip on things.

It can leave us feeling devastated and alone. But praise God, we are not alone. And we are not beyond his reach. He is just a prayer away. When life pushes you with your back against the wall, just raise your hands in total surrender to God, and let him carry you through your troubles. We are only in the beginning of trouble. The worst is yet to come. Sometimes, those that are the closest to us hurt us the most. We are living in a very godless society. But there are still a handful of us Christians that are still here. And we are pushing back the darkness and letting our light shine. Let the glory of the Lord rise upon you.

> Arise, shine; for thy light is come, and the glory of the Lord is risen upon thee. For, behold, the darkness shall cover the earth, and gross darkness the people: but the Lord shall arise upon thee, and his glory shall be seen upon thee. (Isaiah 60:1, 2 KJV)

The enemy of our souls cannot go beyond his limit. God allows the enemy to go so far. For he cannot do what he wants to us. Trouble comes to us all. But what we do with it is up to us. We are not to be afraid of trouble. We must face it with courage. At the same time, we must not be the instigator of trouble. As Christians, we need not fear trouble because we have the whole Army of heaven on our side, and if God is for us, who can be against us?

> The Lord shall fight for you, and ye shall hold your peace. (Exodus 14:14 KJV)

There are always more on our side than those that are against us. Our God will not allow his children to go through more than he knows that they can bear. He knows just how much these frail bodies of ours can take. He will not allow his children to sink beneath the waves of troubles. Before you go under, he will be there to take your hands. When you are face-to-face with trouble of some kind, just call upon Jesus. He is right beside you, waiting on you to call out to him. When we are experiencing some kind of trouble, we just want to shut ourselves out from the world. But that is the time that we need to be around people.

And remember that trouble is not in your life to stay, only Jesus. When we go through trouble, it is very important to know that we are never alone. God is always very near us. The forces of evil would love to make us think that God has abandoned us. But that is just not true. We can call on him anytime, day or night, and he will answer.

He is waiting to rescue his suffering children from all that they are struggling with. These times that we are living in are full of trouble. And there is no place that we can go to escape it. We are safe only in the loving arms of Jesus. When you find yourself surrounded by trouble, look up and say, "Jesus, please see me through this as only you can."

Trading Earth for Heaven

One day, we will walk on streets of gold. One day, we shall never grow old. One day, we shall sit at the Master's feet, and O what a wonderful threat. One day, the roll will be called for one and for all. And one day, there'll be no more curse upon this universe. So whatever you are going through at the moment, remember that this, too, shall pass. This won't last. Because one day, heaven will be ours at last.

CHAPTER 17

✦✦✦✦✦✦✦✦✦✦✦✦✦✦✦✦✦✦✦✦✦✦✦✦✦✦✦

Living on Borrowed Time

We are living life as though this world has no end, living only for the here and now. God has given us all a short amount of time on earth. And what we do with it is very important. Time is a very precious commodity. And we must use it wisely. We are all living on borrowed time. We don't know when we will take our last breath. Probation for each of us could close at any moment. We each have twenty-four hours in a day. Jesus wants us to use that time for eternal things. He knows that we have to raise a family, work, and do other things. He wants us to also enjoy the life that he has blessed us with. But we must also remember that living for the here and now is like putting your money in a sack with holes. But when we live with eternity in view, then we are careful how we use our time from the rising of the sun until it sets. We should be living a life that glorifies God, making every precious moment count for his glory. We are also living in a world of so much distractions. It's all around us. And the purpose for that is to keep us occupied and distracted so that we are not aware of the time slipping away from us, and before you know it, we are standing before the throne of God with no explanation on how we wasted our time on earth.

Jesus wants us to be alert and aware of all the snares of the enemy. For he will stop at nothing if he knows that our soul will be lost in the end. You must not give him that opportunity. You must make the right choice in choosing to let God be your guide. Time is fast coming to an end. And how you choose to spend it will decide your destiny. Always live with the thought that whatever you are doing, thinking, seeing, or speaking is for the glory of God. When we find ourselves drifting away from the right path, then we must quickly return to God, and seeking his help and guidance, we must let him put us back on the right path. God has eternal life waiting for you and me. He does not want us to be caught up in the snares of the enemy and in the process lose our soul. Remember, we are all living on borrowed time. So let us make good use of the time we have left.

Calling on Jesus

When I don't know how to pay my bills, I call on the one who owns the cattle on the thousand hills. Then I am reminded to just be still. And wonder of wonders, my heart is thrilled as the Master pays all my bills. Don't take a pill, so you can chill. Just wait on the Lord, and he will reward.

CHAPTER 18

✕✕✕✕✕✕✕✕✕✕✕✕✕✕✕✕✕✕✕✕✕✕✕✕✕✕✕✕✕✕✕✕✕✕✕✕✕✕✕

Hope for the Future

I know that we are living in some very fearful times.

> Men's hearts failing them for fear, and for looking
> after those things which are coming on the earth:
> for the powers of heaven shall be shaken. (Luke
> 21:26 KJV)

God doesn't want his children to live in fear. And he wants us all to trust him even when we don't know what lies ahead. We don't know what our future holds, but God knows, and that is good enough for me. God is not going to leave us in this world of chaos and confusion to fend for ourself. This world may seem to be out of control, but our God is not. He has everything under perfect control. We try to find peace and happiness in all kind of ways. We hear the nations all around talking about peace and hope for the future. But they cannot give what they themself don't have.

Only God can keep all his promises to his children. And he has promised that he has a bright future and hope for all those that choose to serve him (Jeremiah 29:11 KJV). Sometimes, when we are experiencing hard times and dark days, the future seems to be bleak and hopeless. But if we could trust God in the midst of those times and rest upon his promises, knowing that he is faithful, then and only then we are assured of a bright future. There is no future for those that have chosen to turn their back on Jesus. This world is all there is for them. Jesus came to set us free from the bondage of sin. He paid the price in full for you and me so that we could have hope and a bright future.

In this world of sin, we have only heartaches, pain, sorrows, disappointments, and discouragement, and the end of all that is death. But if we are living for Jesus, at the end of this life, there is a future that has no end. And Jesus himself will be there with us. So whatever we are going through in this life, and if we are walking with Jesus, then we don't have to worry. God is not going to leave us for a second.

> Let your conversation be without covetousness; and be content with such things as ye have: for he hath said, I will never leave thee, nor forsake thee. (Hebrews 13:5 KJV)

> And I give unto them eternal life; and they shall never perish, neither shall any man pluck them out of my hands. (John10:28 KJV)

These times that we are living in are times that Jesus warned us about long ago. This world is full of trouble, and the human heart is growing colder and colder by the minute. Let us not get so caught up in all that is happening that we miss out on being ready to spend eternity with the one that loves us so very much.

Jesus has promised us that he has gone to prepare a place for us, and he will come again to take us to be with him. That, my friend, is a future out of this world. And I am looking, longing, and waiting for that bright future, a future where satan and sin will never show their ugly head ever again. So if you want to have a secure and safe future, stay on God's side. And if you don't know him, please get to know him soon. Give him all your cherished sins, repent of them, and ask him to come into your heart today before it is forever too late. Then you can have hope for your future.

Life Is but a Vapor

The rich, the poor, the young, and the old, death calls to them all. Today, we stand tall. Tomorrow, we crumble and fall. To one and to all, the roll will be called. So get rid of your hate if you want to enter those gates.

CHAPTER 19

<><><><><><><><><><><><><><><><><><><><><><><><><><><><>

A Mother's Prayer

Mothers, please don't stop praying for your children. I am the product of a faithful, praying mother. I am sure there were times she must have thought that her prayers were of no avail. But she kept them going for me anyhow, and not just for me but for all of her children. Day and night, I would see my dear mother on her knees interceding for those she loves so much. There were eight of us, and Mom made the time to pray for each of us by name. Two of my siblings are now asleep in Jesus, waiting for the resurrection morning when we shall all be reunited again. And for the remaining six of us, we are all grown with families of our own. My precious mother is still praying for us and her grandchildren by name. I tell her what a powerful prayer warrior she is because of her consistency in prayer for her children. God has brought me back to the fold of safety.

Today, I am a mother with three kids and grandkids of my own. And I find myself doing the same exact thing as Mother did for me, praying for my children, and the grandchildren, by name, knowing that the same God that heard my mother's prayers for me will hear my prayers for my children and grandchildren. Thank God that he never changes. He is the same always. And he hears the sincere prayers of mothers for their children. So, mothers, please, please, please don't stop praying for your children. And if you are not doing it, please start as soon as possible. Mothers can start as early as when they know that they are expecting. The seed that we plant in the lives of our dear children may not come to bloom until the judgment. But long after we are gone, they will remember and benefit from our prayers.

You may think that your prayers are in vain, and that's just because you don't see the results of your prayers right away and that God is not listening. But God is not a God to ignore the prayers of his helpless children. Remember that we cannot see the wind, but you know that it is there. God is working even when we don't see it. And we must believe that. We must keep our children and grandchildren in prayer now more than ever. We are living in an age where they are being exposed to so much. And for the little ones, their minds cannot prepare them for all that they are being exposed to. That is why we must not waste time. The cry to pray for our children and grandchildren is urgent. We, as parents and grandparents, if we don't take this seriously, we will be losing our kids to drugs, violence, and suicide. And they will leave this world without hope.

We know that even if we pray for our children and grandchildren, bad stuff still happens. That is just the kind of world that we are living in. But we can pray that they are open to the leading of the Holy Spirit and learn to love God for themself. Our prayers for our children will keep them from doing things that they have no business doing. God wants us to keep interceding for our children because he sees all that they are facing. Parents, our children and grandchildren need our prayers more than ever. We must not only pray for protection, but we must plead with God for their salvation most of all. We must be in a constant attitude of prayer for our children and grandchildren. When they are small and in the home, please make sure that you gather them together as often as you can for prayer. And when they are grown, please still pray for them. They need it more than ever because they are facing their own challenges of life.

Our children and grandchildren are our greatest treasures that God has blessed us with. They are only loaned to us for a short time. One day, we, as parents, will stand before God, and he will ask us what did we do with the children that he blessed us with. We must do our part in teaching them about God, and then God will do his part in saving them (Isaiah 49:25 KJV). God said that he will save our children if they allow him to do so. Parents, please don't get weary or discouraged in praying for your children and grandchildren. You will reap a harvest of reward if you faint not.

We are called to pray for our children and grandchildren. We plant the seed, and God will water it and make it grow. As parents, we have a great responsibility to God for our children and grandchildren. So let us continue in being mothers and grandmothers that will pray our children and grandchildren right into the gates of heaven. It is an honor and a privilege to have such an important responsibility. God would not have given it to us if he did not trust us with it. Mothers and grandmothers will go down into history for the great role that they played in raising their children and grandchildren for the glory of God.

Time to Say Goodbye

When it is time for me to go, I wonder how it will be. Will I flee the call, or would I be glad that I am finally set free? A home in heaven is guaranteed for those whose heart is filled with jubilee. The time will come for one and for all, so let us all agree that soon we shall be free. The plea is made for you and for me. It would be wise to open our eyes so we are not caught by surprise.

CHAPTER 20

<><><><><><><><><><><><><><><><><><><><><><><><><><><><><><><>

Trusting God in Our Pain

Pain is a language that we all understand. Some people have emotional pain, some have physical pain, and some have spiritual pain. They all seem to do the same thing. They bring darkness to the soul. There are so many people that are numbing their pain with all sorts of pain medications, trying to escape from the reality of their pain, and there are those that have chosen to do other things. However, one chooses to cope with the pain that they have that will only be a temporary solution.

Jesus is the answer to all our pain. He endured the most pain ever. No one on this earth will ever go through what Jesus went through. He understands when we tell him about our pain whatever it may be. He is near us and wants us to trust him with our pain. Sometimes, we just want it to be a quick fix. Take a pill of some kind, and then the pain is gone. But sometimes, it is more than just taking a pill.

Pain is a way that God is sometimes trying to get our attention and letting us know that he cares about the body that he has blessed us with. Sometimes, we treat our bodies like they are machines. But even machines break down. Our health is very important that once it goes, no matter how much money you have, if you are in poor health, money is of little to no value to you.

I personally live with chronic back pain twenty-four hours a day. It is truly no fun. But during those dark and painful times, I find myself calling on my dear Jesus more and more. For me, it has brought me closer to God. I find him to be my best friend. He understands just what I am going through, and he deeply cares.

> And he said unto me, My grace is sufficient for thee: for my strength is made perfect in weakness. Most gladly therefore will I rather glory in my infirmities, that the power of Christ may rest upon me. (2 Corinthians 12:9 KJV)

And he gives me the strength to endure.

Pain is inevitable. You cannot avoid it. And it has no respect of person. It comes to one and all, the young and the old. But when we choose to trust God with our pain, then we can have a more better outlook on our pain. God may choose to leave the pain, but he will allow you to endure and to learn from your pain. Nothing comes to us just for the sake of it.

With God, All Things Are Possible

> If you are disable, God is well able. If you are weak, God is unique, God has all power, and he will help you in each hour. If you are lost, just remember the cross. If you are lonely, he is your one and only.

CHAPTER 21

<><><><><><><><><><><><><><><><><><><><><><><><><><><><><><><>

Choosing Sides

We are making choices every day of our lives. Some are the right choices, and some are the wrong ones, but no matter what kind of choices we make, they will have an impact on our life for good or for bad. We are living in a great controversy between good and evil. There is a battle raging for the human soul. And every day that goes by is a day that we have chosen to be on one side or the other. Standing on the right side of life means that you have chosen to stand on God's side. And if you do that, all the forces of hell will try their best to discourage you. But remember that God is greater than anything that comes against you.

Each day, you will be faced with which side to choose from. Choosing to stay on God's side is the only way to go. You will hear God's voice speaking clearly to you if you are listening. He is pleading for your soul. Please don't choose the other side. God paid a dear price for your soul. And he wants you to spend eternity with him. Please choose to stay on God's side, the winning side. Please let the voice of God be the loudest voice that you hear. The other voices do not matter. Choosing side is a matter of life and death. Eternal life, and the second death, is what we have to choose from.

> I call heaven and earth to record this day against
> you, that I have set before you life and death,
> blessing and cursing: therefore choose life, that

both thou and thy seed may live. (Deuteronomy
30:19 KJV)

God's voice is the only one that you should really be listening to.
God understands that we are in a battle and that the struggle is real.
He will equip us with just what we need to live the Christian's life.
He knows that we are weak and that we are no match for the forces
of evil. But when we choose to be on God's side, then we can face the
evil ones in the mighty and powerful name of Jesus, the name that is
above all name, and that at the precious name of my Jesus, every knee
shall bow. So today, I pray that you will make the choice to stay on
God's side, to let him be your guide all through life, and then when
at last you see him face-to-face, you will see that you have made the
right choice. God is not going to make you choose his side. He does
not force anyone. God is love, and all that follows him must do it out
of love for him. His love will give you courage to live for him.

God wants each of us to make the right choice. And that is to
live for him. His interest for us is only good. He cares deeply about
our eternal destiny. When we make the choice to go against God,
we have made a very sad choice. At one time or another, we have all
made that choice. But thanks be to God that some of us repented
and turned back around to God. And because of his great love for us,
he accepted us back. Choose this day who you will serve because by
your choice, you have decided the destiny of your future.

> The Lord is not slack concerning his promise, as
> some men count slackness; but is longsuffering
> to us-ward, not willing that any should perish,
> but that all should come to repentance. (2 Peter
> 3:9 KJV)

He has done all that he can do so that the human race can have
eternal life. All we have to do is choose it. He will not make you
choose. God wants you to do it of your own free will. Once you have
made the choice to follow him, then he will empower you to walk in

his ways. But the choice is yours to make. Please don't delay. Do it today. The life you save will be your own.

The Heavenly Flight

I live each day in anticipation, knowing that heaven soon will be my final destination. Thank God for his invitation. We are waiting for the grand celebration that will end all of life frustrations.

CHAPTER 22

◇◇

The Unfairness of Life

When it comes to life, it is anything but fair. Sometimes we can go through some very bad and painful situations that can leave us with some pretty bad memories. People can hurt us, and they do hurt us deeply. And sometimes, you don't have to do them anything. The unfairness of life can leave us discouraged, disappointed, and downcast. But we need not be because while life is so unfair, God is not. Our God is righteous and faithful. He gives us all what we don't deserve.

> That ye may be the children of your Father which
> is in heaven: for he maketh his sun to rise on the
> evil and on the good, and sendeth rain on the just
> and on the unjust. (Matthew 5:45 KJV)

People sometimes get away with terrible things, while others seem to suffer for doing nothing. Sometimes, we are treated differently just because of the color of our skin or because we look different. The unfairness of life is not something new. It is as old as time itself. But as we near the end of this life, things are going from bad to worse. That is why we are not to put our trust and confidence in man. They are sinful beings and do make mistakes.

> But the end of all things is at hand: be ye therefore
> sober, and watch unto prayer. (1 Peter 4:7 KJV)

The unfairness of this life, thank God, will not follow us into the next if we have made Christ Jesus our eternal hope. When things go wrong in our life, we don't seem to blame the enemy for the bad things in our lives. We blame God. And that is so unfair.

> He said unto them, An enemy hath done this.
> The servants said unto him, Wilt thou then that
> we go and gather them up? (Matthew 13:28 KJV)

Jesus said an enemy has done this.

There is unfairness all around us. People take advantage of others, working them like mules and paying them little to nothing. The rich takes advantage of the poor. People suffering at the hands of other people and children that are at no fault of their own to be in this world, they seem to be the ones that are the most victimized to the unfairness of life. You and I, as Christians, must be very careful how we treat others. We must be like Christ at all times in doing what is right in his eyes and in the eyes of those all around us. It is one thing when the world is unfair, but Christians are to treat people with love, kindness, respect, and fairness. We are not to be like the world in any way. We are called to stand out and be different because one day in the very near future, we will stand in the presence of a holy God and give an account for every act of deeds that we did on this earth. No one will escape that day "for we must all appear before the judgment seat of Christ; that everyone may receive the things done in his body, according to that he hath done, whether it be good or bad" (2 Corinthians 5:10 KJV). When we are in the position to help others, we must do it with fairness to all and not just the ones that we want to be nice to. We must remember the golden rules: Do unto others as we would have them do to us.

When we are the ones being unfair, then we could be sure that someday that same treatment will be done to us. Not just because others are doing it, we must do it. We will all be held accountable individually for our actions. So if you find yourself treating people in a way that does not bring glory to God, repent of it and ask God to help you to be like him in all that you do and say. And he will help you because he wants us to love each other and treat each other with fairness. Yes, life is very unfair, but God is not. So let your motive for living be that of serving others and doing it with fairness.

Eyes of Love

To look upon the one above will let you know that you are love, and his peace will come upon you like a sweet little dove. And when you feel scared, please remember to say a prayer.

CHAPTER 23

<><><><><><><><><><><><><><><><><><><><><><><><><><><><><><><><><>

How to Keep Trusting God in the Midst of a Chaotic World

With our whole world crumbling around us, fear and anxiety seemed to fill the hearts of every person. We wonder if we can trust God. But God is the only one we can truly put our trust in. He has not changed. Only our circumstances and the way of living have changed dramatically. God is not the cause of catastrophes.

> And we know that all things work together for good to them that love God, to them who are the called according to his purpose. (Romans 8:28 KJV)

> To appoint unto them that mourn in Zion, to give unto them beauty for ashes, the oil of joy for mourning, the garment of praise for the spirit of heaviness; that they might be called trees of righteousness, the planting of the Lord, that he might be glorified. (Isaiah 61:3 KJV)

Because of all that is taking place in our world, we seem to withdraw from the only one that can help us during these times. And we focus on the chaos instead of on Christ in the time of chaos. This world is fast coming to its final end. And everything that can be shaken will shake, but if we build our hope and trust in Christ Jesus, then we will be able to stand in these days that we are all facing. Jesus is the answer to all that we are going through if anything, these calamities, and disasters that come upon us should make us trust God even more. These winds of strife are blowing from every direction. And if we can't trust God to see us through this time, we will never be able to survive what lies ahead.

God is a loving God. And he cares deeply for all his created creatures, but especially for you and me. He is a God that can be trusted at all times. We must not only trust him in the good times of our lives. You will find that he is the only friend that you will have during the times of disasters. All may abandon us, but not Jesus. He never leaves our side. When we are facing unexplainable situations, and pain is making life more than bearable for us, we are to turn to the only one that understands what we are going through. You will not find the answer to your sorrows and griefs in a bottle. The only way out of whatever we are in is to allow Jesus to be our guide and best friend. Who else can we trust with what we are out of control with? My hope and trust are in God. We can trust him in the good times as well as the bad times. He is with us on the mountaintop with the angels, and he is with us in the valley with the demands. He is in full control of all. There is no other that can take the place of Jesus. And no one else can be trusted like him.

We must build our trust not in what we can see but in what we cannot see. Faith that trusts no matter what is faith that is safe and secure. And we do not walk, but what we see and when we trust God through it all, he gives us such peace in the midst of the storm that we face. God allows things to happen so that we can lean more on him and not on ourselves and also so that we can get out of our comfort zone. And sometimes, he allows us to go through hard times to bring us back to him. You may be going down the wrong path of life, and he is allowing things to happen so that you will turn from your sins and turn to him. We think that we have life all figured out, and then we get hit with a pandemic and a worldwide virus. We are left feeling hopeless and helpless. And still, some people think that they have the answer to this epidemic and that they don't need any divine help. The answer to all that this world is facing is Jesus. As we get closer and closer to the end of time, we will be facing more and more disasters, and the heart of all will grow weaker and more fearful as we experience these events that will be taking place. So if you don't have a personal relationship with God, you will not be able to endure. And if you are already walking in the ways of our Lord Jesus, then you know that the only wise thing is that you keep trusting him no matter what the outcome is. Through it all, you will find him to be faithful. Can we trust God in the midst of a chaotic world? Absolutely. He is all we have and he is all we need. God is so trustworthy.

The Call of Jesus to All

Judgment soon will fall, so please heed the Savior's call. He bids us all to come because his heart we have won. For you my friends, he paid a dear price, so don't gamble with your life. His love for you will never end, so choose today to be his friend.

CHAPTER 24

◇◇◇◇◇◇◇◇◇◇◇◇◇◇◇◇◇◇◇◇◇◇◇◇◇◇◇◇◇◇◇◇◇◇◇◇◇

Faith vs. Fear

We are living in uncertain times. People's hearts are failing them with great fear. And they are turning to the media instead of reading their Bibles. When we turn to the media, it keeps us in fear and despair. Sure, we must know what is going on around us, but when we are glued to constant bad news, it can affect us in a profound way. How very important is it for us to feed on the Word of God in times like these? We need to have our minds on things that will bring peace and calm our anxiety. And just like we take care of our bodies, the mind is as important. We must feed the mind the right thing, or it will not function properly, leaving us in a fearful and anxious state. (You are what you think.)

When we fill our minds with the things that will keep us in fear, then we have to rely on strong medications to help us cope with the constant anxiety attack that comes our way. Our dear Lord Jesus does not want us to live like that. He offers to one and to all his perfect peace.

> Come unto me, all ye that labour and are heavy laden, and I will give you rest. (Matthew 11:28 KJV)

When we do that, then and only then we can face our fear with great faith. When we are seeing trouble through the eyes of the world, then they seem to be bigger than our faith.

But when we see those same troubles in the light of the Holy Word of God, somehow, they don't seem so big after all. The world can only give what it has. And that is much worry, fear, and anxiety. Don't rely on stimulants to get you through the day. But please rely on the Word of God that will get you through all the chaos and catastrophe that we are now facing and for all that is still to come. Fear stops us from going forward. But faith tells us that with God, all things are possible "for God hath not given us the spirit of fear; but of power, and of love, and a sound mind" (2 Timothy 1:7 KJV). Our minds will give us what we have put into it. I think that we, as humans, have one respond to catastrophes, and that is fear. We will all be affected by the events that take place in the world. But you and I must realize that God is bigger than all of that.

And he wants us to have a relationship with him before we face the raging storms of life. God can be trusted at all times. But can he trust us with the circumstances of life? When we have that close relationship with him, he secures us in a circle of his love and seals us as his very own. He knows what he is doing at all times, and when these bad things of life befall us, we must not waver in our faith but be stronger than ever. Gold is not gold until it goes through the fire. We are shining bright stars in a world that is covered with darkness. Christians are to let their light shine and not question if God can be trusted. When we are going through hard times, it lets us know where our faith stands.

As long as things are going well, then we don't know how strong and grounded we are in our faith. God allows us to experience uncomfortable situations so that we can be stretched, and our faith can increase and be strengthened. When we have that closeness with God, and when we take time to be in his holy presence, then these things will not affect us as bad. So please always make your faith bigger than your fear.

His Return

Soon, he will come to take us home and save us
from this life of gloom. To put our trust in him

will save us from this life of grim. The angels soon will sing as we await the coming of our king. The mountains they'll escape, and the earth will be in such bad shape. We shall all have a story, and it will be all for his glory.

CHAPTER 25

<><><><><><><><><><><><><><><><><><><><><><><><><><><><><><><><><><><><><><>

Running the Race Well

Life is a race whether we walk it or run it. Some go at it with all that they have and try to obtain all they can that is of material value. We are all in it to win. And the choice is up to us which prize we want to obtain. If we are only hoping for the prize of life, then our race will be in vain. But if we run to obtain an eternal reward, that, my friend, is the only prize that is worth obtaining. When we are young and full of life, we can do all sort of things, and running the race of life can have little to no meaning for us. We are just going through the motion, trying to survive and make ends meet. But when we are older, we slow our pace down. And then we put things into perspective. We realize that what we thought was so important has now no value at all. We now see life from a different angle, and truly all is vanity under the sun.

All the toys that we accumulated during our lifetime that brought temporary contentment is now a thing of the past. Our lives will be meaningless if we live it without Christ Jesus. We must realize that from the start. And when we get to the end of our life, we will have no regrets. If at the end of our life all we have to show is what we work so hard for, then I think that we have missed the purpose for living.

> For what shall it profit a man, if he shall gain the whole world, and lose his own soul? (Mark 8:36 KJV)

I am not in the rat race of life anymore. God has allowed me to slow down for a reason known only to him. And during this time, I can truly say that I am so much closer to him than I've ever been.

By his grace, my one goal is to run the race well. And at the end of this life, I want to hear my Lord and Savior say to me, "Well done thou good and faithful servant." Those words will be life to me. And that will be a race that was run well. When we are in a race of any kind, no one wants to lose. We all want to obtain some kind of prize. When we finish the race of life, Jesus will give us all a crown of life.

> Looking unto Jesus the author and finisher of our faith; who for the joy that was set before him endured the cross, despising the shame, and is set down at the right hand of the throne of God. (Hebrews 12:2 KJV)

> Being confident of this very thing, that he which hath begun a good work in you will perform it until the day of Jesus Christ. (Philippians 1:6 KJV)

When Jesus is with us, he will allow us to run the race well.

The Cross of Calvary

> As you hang there in shame, you endured much pain because you know that my life would gain much from your pain. So sorry, my Lord, for the pain I caused that nailed your body to that cross. With anguish in your soul, you made me whole. Your love for me is like pure gold. You are mine to have and to hold. And your story, my Lord, shall never, never grow old.

CHAPTER 26

<<<<<<<<<<<<<<<<<<<<<<<<<<<<<<<<<<<<<<<<<<<<<<>>>>>>>>>

In the Blink of an Eye

We tend to take life for granted, not knowing that in the blink of an eye, all could be changed. Life is so fragile and precious, but we don't seem to appreciate it. All that we are and ever will be is because of the goodness of God. Our life is not our own. We are all living this moment because of Jesus. God has blessed us with a certain amount of time on this earth. And he wants us to use it wisely. Things could happen in the blink of an eye. Our life could flash before us, and all the things that we hold so dearly could vanish from us in the blink of an eye.

As I sit here writing, we are in the midst of a pandemic that seemed to happen overnight. People are dying by the hundreds and thousands all around the world. We went from being free and doing as we pleased to a total shutdown worldwide all in the blink of an eye, taking everything that we used to do for granted. Today, we are so restricted. We can't go to church and worship as before. We have to wear a facial mask and be homebound for most of the time. I know that it is for our own safety, but all this took place in such a short time, in the blink of an eye.

A few months ago, if you would have said that we are going to experience a pandemic, I probably would not have believed you. That is why we are to live our lives as though each day is our last because it really can be. In the blink of an eye, we could be no more. Life as we know it could cease to exist. In the blink of an eye, we could be walking down the golden streets of eternity. This life is but a vapor. We must not make our plans, thinking that we are the ones that will make them happen. You do not know what will happen tomorrow. Your life is like a mist.

> Whereas ye know not what shall be on the morrow. For what is your life? It is even a vapour, that appeareth for a little time, and then vanisheth away. (James 4:14 KJV)

In the blink of an eye, we could face a life-threatening situation. We could be overwhelmed by whatever it may be, physical, financial, mental, and emotional. Life is filled with changes and uncertainties that can leave us devastated and defeated. But we are not left without help. Our God has promised that when we put our trust in him, he will keep us in his perfect peace. And we need not let the events that are taking place in our lives, or all around us, defeat us. We must focus only on the good.

> I will lift up mine eyes unto the hills, from whence cometh my help. (Psalm 121 KJV)

So please live your life in anticipation of the soon coming of our Lord Jesus Christ because it could happen in the blink of an eye.

A Mother's Prayer

> My mother's prayers have followed me all through my life. Her tears have touched the heart of God. And her faithfulness in intercessory prayers for all her children has kept them from much harm. Her life of pain and hardship only made her stronger. We are all now grown with children of our own. And Mom is still doing her most amazing thing, and that is praying for her children and grandchildren. I would like to say that it stops there.

But the list goes on and on. As she does what she is called to do. She may not have a clue what her prayers are doing now, but with great joy, she still stops and bow to our heavenly Father up above.

CHAPTER 27

<><><><><><><><><><><><><><><><><><><><><><><><><><><><><><><>

Invisible Chains

When we think of chains, we tend to think of what we could see on the outside. But the invisible ones are the ones that are hidden from the view of all. These chains are chains of the soul. We allow circumstances, one after the other, to lock us up in a place where we cannot express ourself or are not comfortable doing, so we pretend that all is well when on the inside there are invisible chains that are binding us. And we don't know how to deal with them. These chains are something that we carry with us all through our life. They are the childhood scarf. And they can leave us feeling less than complete.

Some cannot live a normal life. Others will occupy themselves with all kind of things, some good and some bad. But they will soon realize that those chains cannot be broken on their own. The invisible chains can be one of many things, abuse of all kind, the death of someone that we love, and the betrayal of a spouse or a friend. These chains that bind us are the snares of the enemy. And we are not to let him enslave us any longer. Christ Jesus is the answer to all that we are dealing with. And nothing is invisible to him. He sees and knows it all. And he deeply cares and wants to help. He is the only one that knows all about us and still loves us so much. We must surrender those chains to Jesus and let him break them. He wants to break every chain that binds us. And he wants to set us free. And whom the Son set free is free indeed (John 8:36 KJV).

He didn't die so that we could still be enslaved to the things that keep us in bondage. Whatever your invisible chains are, give them to Jesus. He is the only one that can make them go away. He knows more than anyone the heavy burdens that you are carrying. And he wants to do the impossible for you and me. When we allow Jesus to have those invisible chains, he takes them and break them like flax of ropes. They may be weighing us down, but they are nothing for Jesus. He will work them all out for his glory and our good. Invisible chains can bring invisible pain. We all have something that we are uncomfortable with, and we think that it's better to hide them away on the shelves of the soul where no one can see them. In the meantime, we are miserable with ourself. We want to be free, yet at the same time, we don't want to talk about those chains.

Please know that you can trust God with your deepest pain. We could be free on the outside but very much in chain on the inside.

> The thief cometh not, but for to steal, and to kill, and to destroy: I am come that they might have life, and that they might have it more abundantly. (John 10:10 KJV)

As long as we hold on to those invisible chains, we will be in bondage to them. You may be a victim to those invisible chains, but God wants to make you a victor. You can be a living witness to others and tell them how God has set you free from your invisible chains, and he could do the same for them.

The Eyes of God

> The injustice of life will never prevail because God sees it all in every detail. Sin and its sorrows will not follow me into that bright tomorrow. Thank God for his control upon the human soul. To step out of line, one must be out of their mind.

CHAPTER 28

<><><><><><><><><><><><><><><><><><><><><><><><><><><><><><><><><><><>

What Do We Do in the Midst of a Pandemic World

These are some very uncertain times that we are living in. And if we don't know the Lord Jesus, these times could be very crazy for most people. The whole world is in turmoil. And people just don't know what to do. This is not the time to turn on each other but to unite as one for the same cause. And that is to uplift each other. United we stand strong, but divided we fall hard. God is shaking the world up but not to divide the world but that we will draw closer to him and stand strong to fight against the enemy.

> Wherefore take unto you the whole armour of God, that ye may be able to withstand in the evil day, and having done all, to stand. (Ephesians 6:13 KJV)

How can we be more ready for the unexpected situations of life? We can have a personal relationship with our great God, who is in full control of it all. And nothing catches him by surprise, absolutely nothing. When we are resting in his love divine, he wraps us up in his bosom of perfect peace and keeps us safe until the storms of life are passed. But if we don't have him as our shield and our protector, then when we are facing turbulence of many kind, we don't stand a chance.

> God is our refuge and strength, a very present
> help in trouble. (Psalm 46:1 KJV)

It is foolish to think that we can get our own self out of situations that are totally beyond our comprehension. A pandemic is something the whole world has no control over. It may have caught us all by surprise but not Jesus. He is allowing this to happen so that you and I can clearly see who is in full control. We seemed to put Jesus on the back burner of everything. We took him out of our schools, and we took him out of almost everything. Now that we are in a pandemic, facing something that is bigger than us, we are still trying to solve this problem on our own. And only Jesus can take bad and turn it into something good.

Normally, when anything bad happens, the churches are jam-packed. But we are forbidden to go to the only place on earth that can bring some kind of peace and comfort to those that are anxious and afraid. But that should not stop us from turning to God and crying out to him like never before. He is very near to the broken in heart and in spirit. A pandemic is the beginning of our sorrows. This is a wake-up call. The worst is yet to come. We must all stand one day before the judgment throne of God, and on that day, we will have to give an account for all that we did in this life. But our God is a loving and forgiving God. If we make things right with him now, he will erase our sins and remember them no more. He is trying, in a loving way, to get our attention. So he allows catastrophes to come upon us so that we can come back to his tender, loving care before probation close, and there is no more mercy and forgiveness of sin.

This pandemic has truly taken a toll on every one of us. We are entering seven months, and no one thought that it would have last this long. And no one knows when it will end. We will never go back to what normal used to be. We are trying to get used to what seems to be the new normal. But we, as Christians, know that the minute we settle in to be comfortable, then we will be faced with another disaster of some kind. These events must take place, rapidly, and in sequence because the coming of the Lord Jesus is at hand. Everything seems to obey God except the human race. We are such rebellious creatures that God has to take drastic measures to get our attention. He is pleading for you and for me to come home. Please hear his tender plea for your life.

> The Lord is not slack concerning his promise, as some men count slackness; but is longsuffering to us-ward, not willing that any should perish, but that all should come to repentance. (2 Peter 3:9 KJV)

As we are living in this world of pandemic, God promised to see us through these events of life. Let us not lose hope. Our God is on his throne, and he will not forsake his own. His eyes are on each of us. And he knows just how much we can bear. So please trust in him today. And come what may, let him have his way.

The Love of God

> Why you love me so, I would never know. But with great joy, my heart will glow as you teach me how to grow. To walk the straight and narrow path will help me to escape his wrath. The sorrows here below come to me in a row. The love of God will keep my heart aglow.

CHAPTER 29

<><><><><><><><><><><><><><><><><><><><><><><><><><><><>

Staying on God's Side

By God's grace, I have made up my mind to stay on God's side all the way. There are so many challenges that come to us along the way, trying to throw us off the right track. But we must have a set mind that come what may, we will stay true to God. He has been our guide all through this life.

Apart from him, we can do nothing. This life has a lot of bumpy rides, and we are getting ready for the ride of our life. This old earth is soon going to rock and roll like a ship tossed to and fro upon the raging sea. But we are not to be afraid because Jesus is our ship captain, and he will not let the ship sink. We may be tossed to and fro with the troubles and trials that come to us, but if we hold on, we will make it safely to the other side. Our sweet Jesus is not going to leave us behind if we have placed our trust in God. All these roadblocks of life that come to disrupt us and lead us off the heavenly path are snares of the enemy. He wants us to be so distracted that the coming of Jesus will catch us off guard. And then we will be lost. But we are to be aware of all the enemy's schemes. For his time is short, and he knows it. So he is out to conquer and destroy all those that allow him to do so. I have decided to follow Jesus all the way. There is no turning back, no turning back. And though I meet with much trials and tribulations along the way, I will stay on God's side. These are light afflictions for a moment. If you decide to go the other way, you will be so sorry. And you will break God's heart forever because he loves you with an everlasting love. And he really wants to share heaven with you.

Staying on God's side means that we must endure all kinds of things that come our way, turning the other cheek, going the extra mile, and being forgiving to all. The test will be severe and often, but the grace of God help us through it. And he alone can make our enemies to be our footstool. Once you have made up in your mind that you are going to stay on God's side, then you can expect to face much opposition. The enemy has lost a slave, and Jesus has gained a servant.

> And he answered, Fear not: for they that be with us are more than they that be with them. (2 Kings 6:16 KJV)

> Ye are of your father the devil, and the lusts of your father ye will do. He was a murderer from the beginning, and abode not in the truth, because there is no truth in him. When he speaketh a lie, he speaketh of his own: for he is a liar, and the father of it. (John 8:44 KJV)

Our God is victorious over all. Jesus is not coming back to win a war. He has already won. The enemy is a defeated foe. When Jesus comes again, he is coming to gather his children home. We are his trophies. And he wants to show us off to the whole universe. And staying on God's side is the only way to be. We don't have much time, and the end is very near. So let us all choose to stay on God's side.

Children

> I have three of them. The joy I had in raising them was knowing they are my precious gems. But how happy I would be if they were oh so near to me? I say a prayer for each of them, to the one who sees and care. And even though we are miles apart, they are in my heart.

CHAPTER 30

<><><><><><><><><><><><><><><><><><><><><><><><><><><><><><><><><><>

Holding On

Sometimes people will say to us, "How are you doing today?" And in these times that we are facing, we will reply, "I'm hanging in there." But the truth is we are holding on to God's powerful hand. And he is holding our hand with a grip that nothing or no one can snatch us away. Giving up is easy. But holding on takes strength and much courage. When we are faced with oppositions of many kind, the temptation will be to give up and quit. And that is just what the enemy wants us to do. Please determine in your mind that you will take hold of God's hand, and you will never let it go. No matter how bad things get, giving up is not an option. At the moment, you can only see hardship, but if you keep holding on, you will be greatly rewarded. Sometimes, we do so much for others, and what we do seems to go unnoticed. If we are doing what we do to draw attention to ourselves, then that will be the result most of the time. People are humans, and they will fail us every time. But if we are doing it for the glory of God, then great is our reward.

> And let us not be weary in well doing: for in due season we shall reap, if we faint not. (Galatians 6:9 KJV)

Holding on and not giving up is a challenge. But we are not doing it in our own strength. It is the power of God that is holding us safe and secure. God is with us each and every step of the way. We are in good hands. We are in the hands of Jesus. There is nothing in this world worth holding on to. Whatever we have, we must hold it with an open hand because it is of little value. Grab a hold of the Master's hand, and please don't let it go. Allow him to be your guide through life. And when it is all over, we shall be with our dear Lord Jesus forever. Some people can hold on while the going is good, but when it gets rough and tough, then they find that holding on is too hard. God did not promise that life will be the rose without the thorns. It's the thorns that make us or break us. And sometimes God has to break us before he can make us whole. No one likes the breaking. We all just want to get through life with little to no hardship. Life is hard from the womb to the tomb. And not one of us will escape the trials and suffering that we must go through. But how much easier it is when we can hold on to the Savior's hand and know that he is going to take good care of us? So whatever you are tempted to do, please don't let go of Jesus's hand. Hold on with all you have.

Siblings

They are good to have. Although we're not the same, we bear each other's pain. When one is weak and drained, the others don't complain. We stand together like a chain. That always will remain. We are connected to each other like a rudder.

CHAPTER 31

◇◇◇◇◇◇◇◇◇◇◇◇◇◇◇◇◇◇◇◇◇◇◇◇◇◇◇◇◇◇◇◇◇◇◇◇◇

Spiritual Warfare

For those people that don't believe in spiritual warfare, that could only mean one thing, that they are on the same side as the enemy. If you are not facing oppositions of some kind, then you and the enemy are walking side by side. For he will not hate his own. For he only hates those that are on the side of Christ Jesus. The more oppositions you have, the closer is your walk with the Lord Jesus. The battle is real, no doubt about it. This is a battle for the soul and mind of the human race. And this battle begins in the mind. If the enemy can control our minds, then he can control us. But we must not just sit and do nothing. If we are children of the most high God, then we have no need to fear this battle. It's up to us which side we choose to be on. The side that we choose is the side that we will serve.

> Know ye not, that to whom ye yield yourselves servants to obey, his servants ye are to whom ye obey; whether of sin unto death, or of obedience unto righteousness? (Romans 6:16 KJV)

The mind is the central station for the battle. Whatever you allow your mind to think, that will tell you whose side you are on.

> And be not conformed to this world: but be ye transformed by the renewing of your mind, that

ye may prove what is that good, and acceptable, and perfect, will of God. (Romans 12:2 KJV)

We are not the enemy's doormat; he cannot do to us as he pleases. We have the whole Army of God on our side. And there is no way that evil can prevail against God's children.

Ye are of God, little children, and have overcome them: because greater is he that is in you, than he that is in the world. (1 John 4:4 KJV)

Finally, my brethren, be strong in the Lord, and in the power of his might. Put on the whole armour of God, that ye may be able to stand against the wiles of the devil. For we wrestle not against flesh and blood, but against principalities, against powers, against the rulers of the darkness of this world, against spiritual wickedness in high places. Wherefore take unto you the whole armour of God, that ye may be able to withstand in the evil day, and having done all, to stand. Stand therefore, having your loins girt about with truth, and having on the breastplate of righteousness; And your feet shod with the preparation of the gospel of peace; Above all, taking the shield of faith, wherewith ye shall be able to quench all the fiery darts of the wicked. And take the helmet of salvation, and the sword of the Spirit, which is the word of God: Praying always with all prayer and supplication in the Spirit, and watching thereunto with all perseverance and supplication for all saints. (Ephesians 6:10–18 KJV)

Every part of that armor is very important. We must not leave any area uncovered because then that becomes a loophole for the enemy. When we are fully equipped with the armor of God, then we are ready for battle. Don't, by any means, think that you can face the forces of evil on your own. We are no match for them. They don't fear us. They fear and tremble at the great God that we serve. When the enemy comes knocking at your door, like a little child, we can say, "Daddy, someone is at the door." Our heavenly daddy will open the door, and no one will be there. Spiritual warfare will be going on until this great controversy has ended. And our Lord Jesus has come to put an end to sin once and for all. But until then, we will have to face the enemy head-on, knowing who is on our side and that God wants us to be brave soldiers in his Army.

> Have not I commanded thee? Be strong and of a good courage; be not afraid, neither be thou dismayed: for the Lord thy God is with thee whithersoever thou goest. (Joshua 1:9 KJV)

> Let your conversation be without covetousness; and be content with such things as ye have: for he hath said, I will never leave thee, nor forsake thee. (Hebrews 13:5 KJV)

> What shall we then say to these things? If God be for us, who can be against us? (Romans 8:31 KJV)

We know that the forces of hell are against us. But they will not prevail. King Jesus is victorious, and he will never leave us in the hands of the evil ones. We are his treasures. So please guard your mind carefully because that is the battlefield. And we, as Christians, will fight all of our battles on our knees. The nearer that we get to the soon return of Christ Jesus, the more intense the spiritual warfare will be. But just as Jesus was with those that went on before us, he will be with us. Please stay true and faithful. The battle is almost over, and the victory has already been won! Our Lord Jesus Christ is coming back to claim his prize. That is you and me if we stay true and faithful. In these last days, we will suffer greatly for the cause of Christ, but please don't let him go.

> Fear none of those things which thou shalt suffer: behold, the devil shall cast some of you into prison, that ye may be tried; and ye shall have tribulation ten days: be thou faithful unto death, and I will give thee a crown of life. (Revelation 2:10 KJV)

> And ye shall tread down the wicked; for they shall be ashes under the soles of your feet in the day that I shall do this, saith the Lord of hosts. (Malachi 4:3 KJV)

But until that day, we must bravely face the foe. God is for us, God is with us, and God is in full control.

The Beauty of a Rose

My little Scarlett rose is sweeter than a pose. To touch her little nose makes her jump to her toes. To hear her giggle from heart, it makes me never to depart. The twinkle in her eyes, it tells me she is very wise. The smile and giggle of a child will make you go the extra mile. The joy and peace it brings to me to have her sit upon my knee.

CHAPTER 32

<<<<<<<<<<<<<<<<<<<<<<<<<<<<<<<<<<<<<<<<<<<<<<<

Trials and Tribulations

> My brethren, count it all joy when ye fall into
> divers temptations;3 Knowing this, that the try-
> ing of your faith worketh patience. (James 1:2–3
> KJV)

> Yea, and all that will live godly in Christ Jesus
> shall suffer persecution. (2 Timothy 3:12 KJV)

For the believers, suffering is inevitable. We will not escape it. Trials
are no fun. But we are to count it all joy when we are going through
them. It does not mean that we are going to be laughing and jumping
for joy because we are going through some very painful situations.
We are human, and humans have feelings.

Some people think that because we are Christians, we are not
supposed to be in pain of any kind or we are exempt from trials. We
will go through the same as the unbelievers, but how we deal with it
is what really matters. Trials come in many forms, shapes, and sizes.
They have two purposes, to break you down to nothing or build
you up and make you stronger. You have the choice of what you will
allow the trials to do to you. The temptation will be to quit, but what
will you accomplish by doing that? You will have missed an opportunity to learn and grow from the trials. God is our great teacher. And

like any good teacher, he will allow us to take the test over until we pass it. It does not give him joy when we are going through trials. But he knows the benefits that come from them. And he is allowing trials to come to his children to prepare us and fit us for heaven.

It is very important for us to remember that when we are passing through the fiery furnace, we are not focusing on the trials but on the one that is bigger and stronger than any trial that we face. God is the mighty God of the universe.

> He telleth the number of the stars; he calleth
> them all by their names. (Psalm 147:4 KJV)

He spoke this world into existence. He is a great and mighty God.

> And the Lord God formed man of the dust of the
> ground, and breathed into his nostrils the breath
> of life; and man became a living soul. (Genesis
> 2:7 KJV)

Of all his created creatures, we, as humans, are his favorite of all. He spoke everything else into existence, but he loves us so much that he took the time to create us. He left the splendors of heaven to come to this cesspool of sin to die for you and me.

He loves us so much that he risks all of heaven for us. He knows the road that we must take. And he knows that it's the road of suffering. Trials are what the Christians need to keep us like Christ. He knows more than anyone, what suffering is all about. And all that have chosen to walk in the Master's footsteps must walk the path of suffering. We are not to shun that path at all or be afraid of it. Some have been put to death because they have decided to stay on the path of suffering for their Lord Jesus. And we should be no different, honoring our dear Savior with all that we have even if it is to our death. And then he will reward us with a crown of life. So I say to one and to all, don't despise your trials, but instead, count them as joy. It is an honor to suffer for Jesus, who suffered so much for us first. If we stay true and faithful to him, he will turn our trials into great triumph.

> For his anger endureth but a moment; in his favour is life: weeping may endure for a night, but joy cometh in the morning. (Psalms 30:5 KJV)

Pain

To live with pain is like the rain. It falls and falls until you're drained. One day, I shall gain a life without no pain. But as for now, I shall not complain.

CHAPTER 33

<><><><><><><><><><><><><><><><><><><><><><><><><><><>

Perseverance

God's children are not to ever give up. When we come to him with our petitions, and we don't get our answer right away or in the time that we want it, we should not stop praying. We must be like the persistent widow, who refused to give up.

> And he spake a parable unto them to this end, that men ought always to pray, and not to faint; Saying, There was in a city a judge, which feared not God, neither regarded man: And there was a widow in that city; and she came unto him, saying, Avenge me of mine adversary. And he would not for a while: but afterward he said within himself, Though I fear not God, nor regard man; Yet because this widow troubleth me, I will avenge her, lest by her continual coming she weary me. And the Lord said, Hear what the unjust judge saith. And shall not God avenge his own elect, which cry day and night unto him, though he bear long with them? I tell you that he will avenge them speedily. Nevertheless when the Son of man cometh, shall he find faith on the earth? (Luke 18:1–8)

We must not pray only once. Sometimes, God answers our prayers instantly. And there are times that he may delay. But he knows just what he is doing. He is never early, and he is never late, but he is always on time. And his delays are always for our good. Even a little child knows the meaning of perseverance. If they have their eyes on a particular object, and they really want it, you will hear from them night and day until you give in and buy it for them.

God wants to increase our faith. When we ask him for something, and we have to wait.

> Ask, and it shall be given you; seek, and ye shall find; knock, and it shall be opened unto you. (Matthew 7:7 KJV).

We must not do it only one time. We can never exhaust or weary God with our asking. He is delighted and honored when we persevere in our request to him. The key is never to give up. Whatever you are asking for, if it is lined up with his will for your life, then he will allow you to have it. But if you are asking for something that will harm you or someone else, then you may not receive it. Always say, "Thy will be done." That way, you are not disappointed if the answer is no.

God knows just what is best for us. We must trust him and know that he will give us what will glorify him and be a blessing to others. Parents are not to be quick to give up on praying for their children. We must pray for our children until we don't have any breath left in us or until the Lord comes. When our children are small, our duty for them is to give them the basic necessities of life. But when they are grown, the need is different. They need our prayers more than ever.

We must persevere in prayer for them until we see a breakthrough. Don't get discouraged if you are not seeing any changes. God is hearing all your prayers. And he is storing them up into heaven's storehouse for the appointed time. Sometimes, he could answer right away, and sometimes, it could take decades. But time to God is not the way time is to us. Twenty years to God could be like a second. Our job is not to get weary in doing good.

> And let us not be weary in well doing: for in due season we shall reap, if we faint not. (Galatians 6:9 KJV)

Nothing that we do for Jesus will ever be in vain. And he wants us to keep praying for our children. He loves them far more than we or anyone else could love them. We cannot take any earthly material possessions with us to heaven. Our children are the greatest treasures that we have. And we should stop at nothing until we see them saved.

> I have no greater joy than to hear that my children walk in truth. (3 John 1:4 KJV)

They are the only treasure that I can take with me to heaven. I will pray for them and my grandchildren until I cannot do it anymore. I know that even when I am long gone, my prayers will follow them wherever they go. As parents, we are not to give up. This is very important. We are talking about life and death, heaven or hell. We must care about the salvation of our children and where they will spend eternity. This topic for me is very important. That is why I wrote it in two chapters of this book.

So if you want to persevere at anything in life, please persevere at keeping your children before the throne of God day and night. You will be greatly rewarded, and they will spend eternity with our loving heavenly Father. Yes, heaven will still be heaven if they are not there. But how much more sweeter heaven will be when we see our children, grandchildren, and all those that we love there? Please don't stop praying for your children. God sees, God hears, and God really cares about our children more than we do. We are all familiar with the acronym PUSH. We are to *pray until something happens*. In other word, keep on persevering.

Jesus

There is no name like Jesus, who can rule the mighty universe, which caused him to be cursed. His love for you and me has made us to be free. Sin demands blood from me, but Jesus stood upon that tree. To turn away from him is to ignore his plea. His nailed hands and feet are more than enough to make me weep.

CHAPTER 34

<><><><><><><><><><><><><><><><><><><><><><><><><><><>

Total Surrender

I have some health issues, and there are days that it's hard for me to get anything done. I was a very independent person. For me, the word *surrender* meant "defeat." It was very hard for me to learn that *surrender* means "to let go and let God." When I learned that I had no control over my situation, then I realize that God is the only one that can walk me through this journey. He will be my guide, and he knows what lays ahead.

> Come unto me, all ye that labour and are heavy laden, and I will give you rest. (Matthew 11:28 KJV)

He wants me to trust in him at all times and to know that he is in full control. Whatever is over my head is under his feet.

Sometimes, I still find myself trying to do impossible things that I know I cannot do. Then he whispers to me gently, "My child, you need to surrender that to me." In frustration, I find myself weeping at his feet, surrendering my impossible task to him. And then I feel like a bird that was set free. Surrender is a daily task. We are always going to be overwhelmed by circumstances beyond our control. And before they get the best of us, let us run to Jesus right away with whatever that is out of our control and surrender it to Jesus. We are good at singing the hymn "All to Jesus I Surrender," but do we really mean it? We may do it for a short time and then go and take it all back whatever it was that we surrendered.

It's not until we have total peace in knowing that our burdens are better in God's hands than on our shoulders. We are not meant to carry heavy loads.

> Cast thy burden upon the Lord, and he shall sustain thee: he shall never suffer the righteous to be moved. (Psalm 55:22 KJV)

Surrendering does not mean defeat at all. It means that you are trusting your life and your future to the all-wise and all-knowing God. When we choose to surrender totally to God, it will save us so much heartache. But because of our pride, we don't want to let go and let God lead and guide. As humans, we all have such strong will to do the wrong things.

But when we choose to surrender that strong will to God, he will use it for his glory and our good. The longer we wait to do so, the longer it will be for us to be free from the burdens that we are carrying. Surrender comes to us as a gift. God gives it to us to free us from carrying loads beyond what we can bear. God knows that we are frail creatures and that the load of life struggles can really weigh us down and rob us of total joy and peace. So he invites us to surrender our heavy loads to him so that we can live the abundant life that he came to give us. So if you are being weighed down by the cares of this life, please let go and let God be your guide. He knows more about our lives than we could ever know. Surrender is not being weak but being wise.

My Journey

Life is a journey. It starts from the womb to the tomb. But in between, there is a lot of gloom. The good news is you don't have to be consumed. God made you a rose so that you can bloom to enjoy their sweet perfume.

CHAPTER 35

<><><><><><><><><><><><><><><><><><><><><><><><><><><><>

Ordinary People

We think that just because we are not in the elite group of life, we are of no value. But that, my friend, is a lie straight from the pit of hell. In the eyes of God, we are all of great value. He thought so much of us when he sacrificed his precious and only begotten Son, Jesus, to take our place on cruel Calvary. Yes, in the eyes of God, we are truly of great value. And we must not allow anyone to diminish our value and worth. We must not look at what others can do that we are not able to do. We all are gifted with heavenly gifts. And remember that God can make ordinary people into extraordinary people.

When you choose to use the gifts that he blesses you with for his glory, we should not try to shine in someone else's shoes. God has made us all unique and special. Each one of us has been given more than one talent, and what we do with those talents is up to us. God is going to hold us accountable for what he knows that we were capable of doing. He will not ask us to do a task that he did not equip us for. But he will expect us to do that which he has enabled us to do. We will be amazed at what God can do with us, to us, and through us. He is the only one that can take you from being the unnoticed to being noticeable and from being the last to the first.

God can do great things through ordinary people. Sometimes, we go unnoticed by other people because we are not doing anything that they can see or they consider is important. But we are not important by what we do. We are very important by who we are and who we belong to. We are children of the most high God. Ordinary people for centuries has allowed God to do extraordinary things through them. One example is Mary, the mother of Jesus. She was an ordinary girl, who allowed the great God of heaven to use her to do something that was so extraordinary, and that was to give birth to our great Savior.

So please don't put yourself down, and think that you are so insignificant that no one cares. Don't live your life trying to please others. Live for Jesus, and that is all that really matters. You will always come up short from the standard of others. People are people everywhere. If you are not in the spotlight of some kind, then you go unnoticed. But remember that people did not died for you, Jesus did. And you are what he says you are—special, unique, beautiful, precious, and extraordinary—and he loves you just the way you are.

A Deadly Virus

There is a virus going around, trying to shut the whole world down. It doesn't matter if you are white or brown. It will surely take you down. But when it's all said and done, a crown of life you have won.

CHAPTER 36

◇◇◇◇◇◇◇◇◇◇◇◇◇◇◇◇◇◇◇◇◇◇◇◇◇◇◇◇◇◇◇◇◇◇◇◇

Waiting for Jesus to Come

As a child, I always heard that Jesus was coming soon. And it always thrilled me to hear about the coming of Jesus. And now as an adult, I know that his coming is much nearer now than fifty-five years ago. The signs of his return are everywhere. Each day and throughout the day, we should all live with great anticipation of seeing Jesus come. We are going from one bad extreme to another. Things are going from bad to worst. And people are going on as usual with their lives. Today is September 9, 2020. And as I sit here, I tell you the honest truth. The day looks like night almost. We have so many wildfires that are burning out of control. And the effect that it has on the environment is so gloomy and dark. There are earthquakes, some other places are having flooding, and others are dealing with all sorts of disasters.

These are truly end-time events. Please let us not get so caught up in all that is happening that we take our eyes off the coming of Jesus. He really is coming soon, and he is trying to get our attention.

> And when these things begin to come to pass, then look up, and lift up your heads; for your redemption draweth nigh. (Luke 21:28 KJV).

These are the beginning of sorrows.

> Watch therefore: for ye know not what hour your
> Lord doth come. (Matthew 24:42 KJV)

We must stay ready, waiting and watching, for the time is at hand.

> And it shall be said in that day, Lo, this is our
> God; we have waited for him, and he will save
> us: this is the Lord; we have waited for him, we
> will be glad and rejoice in his salvation. (Isaiah
> 25:9 KJV)

We are not to sit around idle and doing nothing. We must be occupied with telling others the good news about a loving Savior that loves them so very much and wants to save them all. We have a work to do while waiting for Jesus to come. We must not be content with only seeing our loved ones being saved. We should have a passion for seeing souls come to Jesus. We are saved to serve, not to sit and do nothing. We are the hands and feet of Jesus. And he has equipped us to go out and be his ambassadors to work for him until our last breath or the return of Jesus. And when we get to heaven, our precious Jesus will show us all the souls that are in heaven because we took the time to tell them about him.

Each one of us can do something. We are not all called to go across the continent. We are all missionaries whether faraway or in our own backyard. While we are waiting for Jesus to come, there is still much to be done. Precious souls are perishing each moment as they are going to a Christless grave. Jesus died for all.

> The Lord is not slack concerning his promise, as
> some men count slackness; but is longsuffering
> to us-ward, not willing that any should perish,
> but that all should come to repentance. (2 Peter
> 3:9 KJV)

Our job is to tell them of his great love for them, and it's up to them what they will do with what we have shared with them. Jesus's coming is delayed because he is waiting on you and me to finish the work.

> And this gospel of the kingdom shall be preached
> in all the world for a witness unto all nations; and
> then shall the end come. (Matthew 24:14 KJV)

This we all know that the coming of Jesus is nearer than ever. We are nearing home now more than ever before. I can almost see heaven in view. And I can hardly wait. Each day that God gets me up out of bed, I know that he still has work for me to do. When my work on earth is over, then he will put me to sleep until the glad resurrection morning and until I see his precious face. And then I shall sleep no more. I shall be awakened to a bright and glorious morning where Jesus himself will outshine the sun. And into the land of eternal joy, I shall forevermore explore. The cares of this life are a thing of my past. And heaven at last will be a blast. So what are you doing as you wait for the coming of Jesus? My prayer is that your feet are swift to do his work, and your mouth is ready to speak his love. Your hands are open to give others his word. Stay faithful. Don't look to the left or to the right, keeping your eyes only upward.

> Looking unto Jesus the author and finisher of
> our faith; who for the joy that was set before him
> endured the cross, despising the shame, and is set
> down at the right hand of the throne of God.
> (Hebrews 12:2 KJV)

This is no time to give up or give in. We are nearing home. God promises to reward our faithfulness.

Sunrise

To see the sun rise tells me that there is one who is wealthy and wise and full of surprise. To look upon his eyes makes me feel like I'm his prize. Life has its ups and downs, leaving one with a frown. But thank God that he always sticks around.

CHAPTER 37

<><><><><><><><><><><><><><><><><><><><><><><><><><><><><><><><><>

The Testing of Our Faith

We need faith in all that we do. Our daily existence demands faith. It seems to be easy for us to put our faith in everything else except in the living God. We serve him daily and tell him that we love him. But when he asks us to step out on the limb, then we question him and are hesitant to do what he ask. Hebrews 11:6 (KJV) tells us that, "But without faith it is impossible to please him: for he that cometh to God must believe that he is, and that he is a rewarder of them that diligently seek him." Survival faith is what we have in our daily lives. Such as it takes faith to drive a car, it takes faith to cross the street. It takes great faith to take a pill, not knowing if it will kill you or cure you, yet we take it anyhow. But we have trouble believing in saving faith.

> And Jesus said unto them, Because of your unbelief: for verily I say unto you, If ye have faith as a grain of mustard seed, ye shall say unto this mountain, Remove hence to yonder place; and it shall remove; and nothing shall be impossible unto you. (Matthew 17:20 KJV)

We cannot live without faith.

> For I say, through the grace given unto me, to every man that is among you, not to think of him-

self more highly than he ought to think; but to
think soberly, according as God hath dealt to every
man the measure of faith. (Romans 12:3 KJV)

And today in these last days of earth's history, we need to have
saving faith more than ever. We need to know that God is the only
one that can and will see us through all that we are experiencing in
our world today. Saving faith is placing your whole trust in Jesus
and knowing that he is all who he says that he is and so much more.
Saving faith is God at work. Trusting faith is knowing that God is
working even if we don't see any evidence of it at the moment. We are
to keep on holding on. When we exercise the little faith that we have,
then God will increase it to greater faith. We cannot ask for more
faith if we are not using the faith that we have. When we are worried
and anxious about our daily needs, that is not faith.

In George Müller's book, *Hungry Orphans Fed Miraculously,* he
run his orphanages on faith. There was a time when Mr. Müller had
nothing to feed the children. He sat them all around the table, and
they said their grace. And by the time they said amen, there was a
knock at the door. God had sent a baker with bread for Mr. Müller
and the three hundred children at his orphanage. God honors our
faith when we step out in faith. The Red Sea did not part until the
children of Israel took the step of faith and stepped into the water.
Then that body of water became two walls of water, and they were
able to cross over to the other side. God did not only send bread for
Mr. Müller and the children, but he also send them milk to drink.

We too can have such faith. And it can start with anything.
Our great God is concerned about all that troubles us, big or small.
And when we are asking him for something, we are not to have
any doubt trusting and knowing that he hears all our prayers. God
is not deaf or blind. He sees and he hears all that we are going
through. When we pray for help for ourself or for someone else,
we are to trust that God will work in his time to accomplish his
purpose. And we are to have the faith that he heard our request and
go about our day thanking him for his answer to our prayers even
if they are not yet answered.

(As it is written, I have made thee a father of many nations,) before him whom he believed, even God, who quickeneth the dead, and calleth those things which be not as though they were. (Romans 4:17 KJV)

You will be tested severely and tempted to doubt, but please don't allow anything to weaken or shake your faith. Stand firm in what you believe in. The day will come when your life will be at risk, and you will have to choose your faith or your life.

Please choose your faith. God is able to raise you up again with a glorified, brand-new body. When we are doing something for Jesus, we will be tested severely. Just in writing this book, I was tested severely. The enemy did not want me to do it. But praise God that greater is he that is in me. I knew he had given me an assignment, and he was going to complete what he started in me. I was tested severely. But I know that this is what God wants me to do. So I will persevere by God's grace to the end because I know that my God is greater. And if he allows my faith to be tested, it is for my own good.

We must not let the evil ones think that they can easily discourage us. This journey that we are on is almost at its final end. And more than ever, we will need to rely on the faith that we have in Christ Jesus, faith that can carry us through the storms of this life. If your faith is built on shifting sand, then you have nothing to stand on. But if your faith is built on Christ the solid rock, nothing can shake you. Keep your faith strong and allow nothing or no one to weaken it.

The Coming of Jesus

My Jesus is clear. The hour of his return is drawing near. To one and to all, the plea is made. Don't worry about the price. It's already been paid. Thank you, my king, for everything. Heaven will ring as we sing to our king. With joy and much delight, we will shine bright.

CHAPTER 38

<><><><><><><><><><><><><><><><><><><><><><><><><><><><><><><><>

Interceding for Others

The greatest job that we can do, besides raising our children for Jesus, is to intercede on behalf of others. When we can go before our great God on our knees for others, that pleases Jesus. He wants us to be loving, kind, and caring. Sometimes, people are crushed beneath the heavy burdens that they are carrying. And they need someone to intercede for them. I can't tell you of the many times that I just couldn't pray or read my Bible, and there were many family members and church families that prayed me through those very dark days. So I can testify of the wonderful power of intercessory prays. I do believe that they were used to save my life many times. Some of us have more time than others, and we can spend more time in interceding for others. But even if you seem to have a tight schedule, please make some time to intercede for someone today for someone needs your prayers. And you don't have to look far. It could be in your own family, your neighbors, or someone at work. The whole world needs our prayers.

Intercessory prayers are something that we all can do. It is good not only for the ones that we are praying for but for ourself also. When I tell people that I am praying for them, they oftentimes will say thank-you and tell me how they really appreciate it. And there are times that I would ask an individual if they would like me to pray for them or pray with them, and they would say no. I totally respect that because our God does not want us to force his love on anyone. His love is free to all that accepts it. When we take the time to intercede for others, we show them that they do matter to the great God of the universe. And it tells them that we too care for them. We will be rewarded for what we do for others in the precious name of Jesus "for God is not unrighteous to forget your work and labour of love, which ye have shewed toward his name, in that ye have ministered to the saints, and do minister" (Hebrews 6:10 KJV). We will not be saved by what we do. But we do what we do because we are saved. Our good deeds don't save us. Salvation is through Christ Jesus and him alone.

Interceding for others does not make us better than them. It allows us to partake in a work that perhaps souls will be saved because we have taken the time to pray for them. Our goal should be heaven full and hell empty. When we pray for others, I am reminded of a beautiful hymn in the Seventh-Day Adventist Church, hymnal #505, that goes like this: I need the prayers of those I love while traveling o'er life's rugged way that I may true and faithful be and live for Jesus every day. I want my friends to pray for me to bear my tempted soul above and intercede with God for me. I need the prayers of those I love. This is such a fitting hymn for all of us because we all need the prayers of those we love. God does take notice of what we do for others. And if we are interceding for them, he will greatly reward us. So today, please take the time to intercede for someone.

A Heart That Cries

When the heart is broken with sorrows and despair. We will find it hard to keep back the rolling tears. To bear your burdens all alone will only keep you down and gloom your life of joy and peace. It can consume, but don't despair. There is one who really cares.

CHAPTER 39

<><><><><><><><><><><><><><><><><><><><><><><><><><><><><><><><><><><><><>

Living with Eternity in View

We are all being severely tested with all that is going on around us. Life will never be the same as before. We were forced to change our way of living and thinking because of the pandemic. Many are still choosing to live life without God's guidance. But for those of us that have chosen to continue to stay on the path that we were on before the pandemic, we should not be surprised at all at what is taking place. In the past few months, we have had so many changes to our environment and to the whole world. In the midst of a pandemic, we have numerous California wildfires that are burning all over. The air is so polluted that you can hardly breathe. There are earthquakes in other places and snowstorms in other states. The earth is in her birth pains. We must take all these things that are happening very seriously and live each day with eternity in view, knowing that very soon we could pass from this life to the next.

As Christians, we must live each moment of our lives with eternity in view. We go about doing our daily duties of life. But our hearts and minds are to always be on heaven. We are strangers in a foreign land. This world is not our home. Heaven is our eternal home, and while we are passing through this land, we will be faced with all kind of trials. But we will not be alone. Jesus promises to never leave us or forsake us, and he will not allow us to go through more than we can bear. Whatever the task and whatever the trial, God will see us through it. While waiting to go to our eternal home, we are not to be just waiting. We are to be working hard to win precious souls for the kingdom of God. And together, we can look forward to a better land, a land whose builder and maker is God and sin and satan are never welcome there, a land where our dear Lord Jesus is waiting to welcome us in, and a land where we will call home. That land is heaven. I can hardly wait.

I can truly say that I am homesick for a land that I've never seen before. All I know is that I am tired of trials, sorrows, and so much pain. I want to see my Jesus, throw myself into his loving arms, and ask him why it took so long for him to come, but I know that once I am there, I will not remember my cares and heartaches of this life. I live each day with great expectation in knowing that each day, God wakes me up; it could be the day that Jesus could come or put me to sleep. Jesus said that he does not want us to be caught up in the cares of this life. He wants us to watch and pray so that we are not caught off guard. He knows that there will be so much distractions all around us that will try to take our mind and focus of his soon return. But we are to daily spend time in his presence and not to let the cares of this life be our only focus. Sometimes, we experience difficulties in our life. It could be with our health or just in life general. Whatever it is, we always want a quick fix to it. But God is looking for growth. He wants us to learn from whatever it is that he is allowing to come our way. So instead of praying that God should take away whatever stumbling block that is in our way, we must pray for strength and endurance.

These things that we are facing are only temporary. We are looking and longing for an eternal home. So be brave and courageous. God is with you in all that you go through. And when this life of hardship is finally over, then we will have a life of peace, joy, happiness, and everything good. It will be worth it all when we see Jesus. These trials of life will seem so small when we see Christ. So let us bravely run this race. Be faithful, dear ones, because truly eternity is in view.

No More Shame

Good morning to you, dear. May you know that God is very near to comfort and to cheer. To start your day with him is like the birds that sing. Life is not game, and sin is not a game. My Savior took my blame, so greatly, I'll proclaim the love he has for me is greater than my shame.

CHAPTER 40

<><><><><><><><><><><><><><><><><><><><><><><><><><><><><><><><><><><><><>

Taking God at His Word

> God is not a man, that he should lie; neither the
> son of man, that he should repent: hath he said,
> and shall he not do it? or hath he spoken, and
> shall he not make it good?
> —Numbers 23:19 KJV

When God tells us that he will do something, he will do it. You cannot believe what man says, but God is always true to his word. We have no problem believing in someone that promises us things and does not keep their promises. But when God says to us that he will be our all in all, we have a problem believing that. When he tells us that he will supply all our every needs, we don't believe him. Instead, we tell ourselves that we are the ones meeting our own needs. But what we don't realize is that it is God that blesses us with health so that we can get wealth. God has never gone back on any of his word.

> Heaven and earth shall pass away, but my words
> shall not pass away. (Matthew 24:35 KJV)

The words that God speaks, they instantly become life. They cannot be changed or altered. When we choose to take God at his word, then we are telling him that he has full control over our lives. And whatever he says, we will comply with it. God is looking for people that will see him for who he is, a caring, loving, merciful, and all-knowing God, one that cares about every little detail that troubles his children. He is like a loving father that is just waiting to meet the needs of all his little helpless creatures. We are so blessed and honored to be loved by such a loving heavenly Father. And if he promises to take care of all his children, then he will do just that. We are like the little newborn babies when they are hungry. They just totally depend on the parents to feed them.

> The eyes of all wait upon thee; and thou givest them their meat in due season. Thou openest thine hand, and satisfiest the desire of every living thing. (Psalm 145:15–16 KJV)

God is not a father that creates his children and then turn his back on them as if they don't exist. Only the human fathers do that, not our heavenly Father. We can trust his every word. We can hold his loving hands, close our eyes, and trust our God to lead us wherever he wants to take us and know that we are safe. God will forever be a God of his word.

His Guiding Hands

> Life has many stories that soon one day will end. To know the meaning of my story is to give him all the glory. When we choose to trust his guiding hands, then he reveals to us his plans. To run ahead of him will only bring a life of grim. The only story that has no end is the one that never did begin.

CHAPTER 41

◇◇◇

The Life I Now Live

I am now fifty-five years old. I wish I could say that I feel like a spring chicken, but I don't. I feel like I am closer to the one hundred mark than fifty-five. The journey has been really rough, and there were times that I just felt like I couldn't go on much longer. But in those times, I can truly say that my Jesus carried me through those very dark days. I was not always walking with the Lord. I knew a lot about him, but I did not know him. In my childhood, he was the God of my mother. In my young adult life, he was the God of some of my closest friends. But in my adult life, he became my personal Savior, Master, and best friend. It is through the hardships and trials that I found a loving Savior that has been there waiting for me all along. He has been my guide all through life. But I was too occupied with doing my own thing and living my sinful life that I did not appreciate the guiding hands of the Master. And the many times that I came so close to the edge of the grave, I still did not acknowledge that God had his loving hands on me.

I kept running from him as far as I could go. But no matter where I run, I found that God can run faster because he was already waiting for me wherever I run. We cannot outrun God. And for that, we should be happy. God loves us too much to give up on us. He paid a dear price for us. Every drop of his precious blood was paid to purchase a soul like yours and mine. I had more surgeries in my life than I cared for. But I can truly say that God used each one of them to bring me closer to him. He tried to slow me down in so many ways before. But I did not listen.

C. S. Lewis books, *Desiring God*, said that God speaks to us in our conscience, and we don't listen. He speaks to us in our pleasures, and we still don't listen. But he shouts in our pain. And that was how he got my attention, not just the physical pain but the emotional as well. And that could be worst than the physical pain. As I look back on all the events of my life, I can clearly see the precious hands of my heavenly Father leading and guiding me all the way. It took many years of pain and suffering for me to realize that I needed the Lord. I thought that I could do life on my own, going many years thinking that way. I was always the one that was on the giving end. I would refuse help from all those that offer it to me. I thought that I would become weak if someone help me. I live that way for years.

Today, I can tell you that I am much more humble. I still feel bad at times when it seems like all I am doing is receiving. But the support and help that I get from families and friends are more than I can tell. At first, it was so hard for me to be on the receiving end that I was rejecting the help and, without meaning, offending those that sincerely wanted to help me. I did it one time too many. And one of my sisters said to me, "You are not going to stop my blessings. God wants me to help you, and that is what I will do." So I learned that God works through people. The pain in my back would be so intense at times that I would just weep. But then I turn the focus to my Jesus and know that he suffered much more for me. I praise him in my storms, and somehow, he gets me through each one with a smile. He did not promise us a smooth path to heaven.

> Confirming the souls of the disciples, and exhorting them to continue in the faith, and that we must through much tribulation enter into the kingdom of God. (Acts 14:22 KJV)

No, God did not promise a smooth ride, but he did promise that he will never leave us or forsake us.

So today, I can tell you that the Pearly that I was twenty years ago is not the same Pearly that I am today. I am not perfect, far from it. But my Lord Jesus has brought me from a mighty long way. And I don't mean geographically only. He has seen me through some very hard and painful days. And all that I am today or will ever be, I owe it all to him. As the song says, "To God be the glory for the things he has done for me" (SDA church hymnal #341). He blessed me with a loving family, three children, grandchildren, a daughter-in-law, and one soon-to-be, and a host of my church families that prayed me through some rough times. God has been so good to me that I cannot tell it all. If I had it to do all over again, and the road of pain was the only way that God could get my attention, I would choose that same road again because on that road, I met my Master. And he and I became best of friends. He is mine, and I am his forever and ever.

Nothing on earth matters to me like spending eternity with him. I plead with you today, please don't wait until the bottom falls out of your bucket to turn to God. He is trying in so many ways to get your attention. And he will do anything to get it. If you have to hit rock bottom, and the only thing that you can do is look up, then you will realize just like I did that God has been there all along, waiting for you to acknowledge his presence. My dear ones, time is really short. And Jesus is soon to come. We must decide today that we want to be on his team and ask him to come into your life and be the Lord and Master of your soul. He so wants to do that. Won't you please let him into your heart? Oh, how he wants to come in. He loves you so very much. And heaven will forever have an empty space where you should have been if you are not there. And there is no need for that. The price has already been paid for you.

All you have to do is accept it. Please don't listen to the lies of the enemy. He will tell you that you have plenty of time and that you don't need to live for Jesus now. Have fun, and live it up. Those have been his lies for thousands of years.

> Ye are of your father the devil, and the lusts of
> your father ye will do. He was a murderer from
> the beginning, and abode not in the truth,

because there is no truth in him. When he speaketh a lie, he speaketh of his own: for he is a liar,
and the father of it. (John 8:44 KJV)

If he could keep you out of heaven, he will. That is his goal. But
greater is he that is in you. Jesus wants you in heaven. Please choose
to live for Jesus instead. God has done all there is to do to save us.
There is nothing more on his part that he can do. He gives us his
all when he gave us his only precious and begotten Son, Jesus. The
choice is up to us now to choose his way. As long as there is breath
in your body, you still have an opportunity to ask him into your life.
Please do it before the door of probation closes. And then it will be
forever too late to make your decision.

While it is said, To day if ye will hear his voice,
harden not your hearts, as in the provocation.
(Hebrews 3:15 KJV)

Do it today. Please don't delay.

A Godly Mother

Our dear mother, she gives us life. She gives us
advice. Her many prayers kept us from strife. Her
love for us has brought us to our knees to call
upon the only one who can make us free. To have
a godly mother that is like no other will be the
greatest treasure that one can uncover.

CHAPTER 42

<<<<<<<<<<<<<<<<<<<<<<<<<<<<<<<<<<<<<<<<<<<<<<<<<<<<<<<<<<<<

Fitted for Heaven

Jesus wants to make us all fitted for heaven if we will allow him to do so.

> A new heart also will I give you, and a new spirit
> will I put within you: and I will take away the
> stony heart out of your flesh, and I will give you
> an heart of flesh. (Ezekiel 36:26 KJV)

To be fitted for heaven, we must let go of earthly pleasures so that we can gain heavenly treasures. If we are being weighed down with the cares of this life, and our eyes are so dim with the mist of tears that we don't see a way out, we must look up and know that God has a way out of our situations. And he is longing for us to turn to him in those times of despair. The heavy baggages of life can steal our joy, peace, and strength. It can leave us without hope. Jesus wants to take all that away from us and make us fitted for heaven. We must be willing to surrender and do whatever it takes to drop those baggages of burdens and allow Jesus to work his perfect will in our life.

We are to walk with him each day and spend much time in his holy word. And as we walk and talk with our dear Savior, he will make us more and more like him. But we cannot get to know him if we are not spending time in his word. His holy word is his love letter to us. If you are not disciplined in that area of your life, you will need to be. Because it is extremely crucial in order to be like him, we must make the time to put him first. How can we be fitted for heaven if we are too occupied with the cares of this world? We are to be more like our blessed Jesus every day. He wants us to be a reflection of him by doing kind and loving deeds to all those around us, but he, most of all, wants us to come into his presence and to have that one-on-one communion with him. Jesus wants us to be like him.

As we go through this life and the many twist and turns that we will take, we must be careful that it does not take us off the right path. Sometimes, when we are experiencing difficulties of some kind, it can make us better or bitter. Always remember that God is not caught off guard by your circumstances. And instead of running from him, please run to him. He is the only one that knows your situations in detail. Your issues of life are no surprise to God. Each day when we face trials and obstacles, we are learning from them. How we react to them is important because others are watching us. And if we trust God, they want to see how well we do under pressure. And if we let God have his way in our pain and suffering, then others can see the power of God through us. It does not mean that we will not shed tears in our pain, but we have chosen to glorify God in our pain. God will have a perfect people at the end of this journey called life. He is coming back for a spotless bride, one that has been fitted for heaven. I want to be a part of his bride. I hope that is your desire also.

This is the end of this book that I called God's little book. We must never underestimate the power of God and what he can do through anyone and for everyone. God can use you if your heart is humble and willing to be used by him. It does not matter if you are educated or uneducated. God calls the unqualified to qualify them for his service. So please don't think that you are insignificant and have no purpose.

> Before I formed thee in the belly I knew thee;
> and before thou camest forth out of the womb
> I sanctified thee, and I ordained thee a prophet
> unto the nations. (Jeremiah 1:5 KJV)

God has a plan and a purpose for all of us. We can all be of service to him. All he need is a willing heart. And he will do his part in leading and guiding you each step of the way. So please give him your heart, and let him surprise you with what he can do with a willing heart, as he did with me. He made the impossible possible. So my precious Master, Savior, and forever best friend gets all the glory, praise, and honor for looking down upon this humble child of his and using her to honor and magnify his most holy name. Jesus is no respect of persons. He can use anyone. And how do I know? Because Jesus used me.

The Bible

Don't be idle. Please read your Bible. To fall on your knees is to know you are in need. When you pray, God will help you to obey. The trials of life can leave us like ice. But don't forget that God paid a high price. His love for us can break the heart ice.

To my precious mother, who spend all her life praying for her children, grandchildren, and many others, I want to say thank you from the bottom of my heart, Mom, for all your prayers. They have guided me through life and will follow me into the next. Your prayers to me are more precious than silver or gold. You taught me how to persevere in intercessory prayer for my own children and grandchildren. The many times that I was so broken and hopeless, you did what you do best. And that was praying for me, and not for me only but for my brothers and sisters as well. I am sure that they can all say the same thing. So, Mom, I say thank you for all you have done for me, but I thank you the most for all your prayers. May God continue to be your guide and personal friend until you see him face-to-face. God bless you, Mom. And I love you dearly.

To my three children, please know that you all are my treasures and the joy of my life. And there is not a day that goes by that I don't pray for each of you. God has blessed me with such amazing children. I am so grateful that he chose me to be your mother. Please stay close to him. He loves you all dearly, and so do I. And he has a wonderful plan for each of your lives.

To my daughter-in-law and grandkids, I love you all. I am so blessed to have you as a part of my family. And to my daughter-in-law to-be, I love you, and I welcome you with open arms in my family. To all my siblings that have seen me in the best of times and in the worst of times and have supported me during both times, I want to say thank you to you all for all your help and support that you have given me throughout my life. We are a whole chain. And if one link is damaged or broken, the others are not content until we are all linked together again. Thank you all so much for everything. I love you all. And may God bless each of you in a special way. Last but not least, to the host of all my nieces and nephews, I love you all dearly, and God bless you all.

It has been such a pleasure in writing this book. I've felt the presence of God more than I have ever felt it in my life. There is nothing like it. I heard his voice so clearly in each one of the chapters and poems. I felt like he was right next to me. I had this sense of great peace when I would sit down to write. The title *Unseen Hands*

That Lead the Way, I heard that so clearly in my head. God wants to use you to do great things for him. And if you would let him, you would be amazed. To one and to all, I say God loves you dearly, and he wants to make your heart his home. Please let him do so.

2020 No More

The year has come to an end. My humble prayer has now begun. Dear Lord, please use me for your glory so that I can share your wonderful story.

Last year was truly a nightmare. Yet your love was seen everywhere. Although the death angel passed through the land, still in mercy you held back your hands. We are glad that 2020 is no more, but only you know what the future holds. To welcome this new year will let us know that God is always near.

When Time Is No More

Soon the long night of time will be ended, and the eternal morning will be presented. And all those that love the Lord will be recommended. No time now to be offended for we shall all be ascended. And when at last his face we see so very happy, we will be. His love for us is pure and free, of that we all can agree.

A Christmas Party

If I wanted to give a Christmas party, what would it look like?

I'll ask the lame, the blind, and the deaf for they would be my honored guests.

I'll seek them out with much delight because to put a smile upon their face will let them know of God's amazing grace.

To help the ones in need will keep me from all greed.

With love for them is what we're here to bring. The joy we share will draw the Son of God so very near, and that my friend will have no end.

Tears No More

Dear Jesus, it is so easy to sit and weep. But life is much sweeter at your feet. To sit around and weep will only make me weak. Oh, how my heart is longing to beat in a land that sin will not repeat. I am most complete when I am at my Savior's feet. His love for me is sure and sweet. And then at last I'll walk on golden streets.

ABOUT THE AUTHOR

Pearly Stanley is the seventh of eight children. Born to Samuel and Lupita, she came to the United States from the country of Honduras, Central America, at the age of sixteen. She thank God for this land of great opportunities where one can become anything they choose to become. She has made it her earthly home until she reaches her heavenly home. God bless the United States of America. She is a mother of three children, a grandmother of one, and a step-grandmother of three young adults. Her hobbies are reading her Bible, cooking, and crocheting. Her passion when she was working was caregiving. She enjoyed that for about twenty-five years. Working with the elderly was more than a passion. It was her calling. She is now in a different season of her life. But she knows that God still have work for her to do because she is still here. God is taking her on a journey that she would not have chosen on her own. But she knows that he knows best, and she chooses to trust him all the way. Her prayers for all those that come in contact with this little book is that you make Jesus the Lord of your life before it's forever too late. God bless you all.

CPSIA information can be obtained
at www.ICGtesting.com
Printed in the USA
LVHW090544261021
701556LV00002B/212